Praise for *Stick with It* and its business impact

"We have successfully applied Colan's powerful tools for 12 years to help drive our business growth and organizational engagement. Stick with It *delivers another clear model and supporting tools presented in Colan's practical and actionable style. We have integrated his thinking into our business, which has been an important factor in our ability to adapt and thrive in the market."*

Barry E. Davis, President and CEO
Crosstex Energy Services

*"*Stick with It *simplifies the complex topic of business execution. We have applied these concepts to create winning business results and a winning culture."*

Paul Spiegelman, CEO
The Beryl Companies

"The Art of Adherence is to Strategy what The Theory of Relativity is to Physics. It's just as compelling but much simpler. Why settle for anything less than eloquent execution and stratospheric success? You don't have to with Stick with It *as your guide book."*

Ronald G. Rossetti, Esq., Associate Vice President,
Trial Division, Nationwide Insurance

"We have applied the concepts from Stick with It, *and we have won! Colan's practical approach makes the hard work of execution very logical, and this book lays it all out clearly and simply."*

Andrew Levi, CEO
Aztec Systems

"Colan is a truly elite corporate coach. Stick with It *delivers invaluable insights into adherence—a common factor for winning leaders. As a result, this book will quickly become a common factor for winning organizations."*

Mark Blinn, CEO
Flowserve

"This book is the secret sauce to being successful with any strategy. Stick with It *is a practical guide for avoiding the very reason that most strategies fail— lack of adherence. The authors bring in real-world and understandable examples that will make you and your organization soar to new heights."*

David T. Feinberg, MD, MBA, President and CEO
UCLA Health System

"The Stick with It *model works in any company because Colan's strategies are grounded in real organizations and in the reality of human nature— not the theoretical. His passion for "keeping it simple" gives leaders confidence they can successfully create positive change."*

Joe Bosch, Chief Human Resources Officer
DIRECT TV

*"*Stick with It *delivers a simple way to tackle a complex problem—execution. This book contains practical tools and insights that help you win on and off the field—in business and in life."*

Roger Staubach, Executive Chairman—Americas
Jones Lang LaSalle Americas, Inc.

"Colan's cut-through-the-clutter approach to strategy enabled us to spend more time on important questions about our business. The art of adherence does the same thing when it's time to put the strategy to work and execute. Stick with It *brings it all together in a quick-read and easy-to-apply format."*

Mike Barnes, Group CEO
Signet Jewelers

"The adherence equation (focus _ competence _ passion) is a powerful formula for driving growth and winning in today's market. Stick with It *balances research with real-world examples to deliver field-tested tools, so you can read it on Friday and apply it on Monday."*

John Walker, COO
KidKraft

Lee Colan is not only a successful businessman, leader, and great verbal communicator—he writes a great book! His simple, clean, and carefully worded prose makes reading this book a joy. Real-world examples provide positive reinforcement for each point made. Simplicity–focus–prioritization–visibility–meeting effectiveness–accountability. Lee handles all of these important issues with wit and clarity. I heartily recommend Stick with It *to leaders and their teams.*

Bryon Potter, Vice Chairman and CEO
DW Distribution

"Persistence and perseverance—to me, two of the most important attributes of a great leader. Lee and Julie provide a wonderful field guide for those committed to developing great strategies and ideas, but most important, executing them with excellence."

Melissa Reiff, President
The Container Store

*"*Stick with It *brings a new level of clarity and simplicity to the age-old challenge of how to achieve outstanding results. Lee's ability to cut through the clutter and give you just the right formula is priceless."*

Cheryl Johnson, Director
Field Human Resources and
Organization Development, ULTA Beauty

"Some books impact your business. Other books change your life. This book does both."

Richard A. Lavinski, CPA, Managing Partner
The SolomonEdwardsGroup

*"*Stick with It *clearly outlines the art and the science of consistent execution. Its rare simplicity and clarity for a business book make it quick to read and easy to apply. The authors build a bridge between knowledge and action that creates a powerful competitive advantage."*

Darron Ash, Chief Financial Officer
Sammons Enterprises, Inc.

"*Stick with It* *is a great book for any company, large or small, or any individual striving for success. It contains a terrific road map on how to win! The timing of this book could not be better because there are so many companies trying to dig out of the recession. I invite everyone to use this book to chart their goals and objectives whether personal or business.*

Larry Foster, Chairman
Foster Financial Group

"*Strategy is the fuel to survive, and flawless execution is how you thrive. Fill your tank with this superb book and reenergize your leadership journey.*"

Robert J. Bunker, Chairman and CEO
Medical Staffing Network LLC

"*At a time when clutter, fast-changing priorities, and obsessive doubting seem to be the norm,* Stick with It *provides the most practical blueprint for achieving business and personal success that I have ever seen. This is a 'must read' book for every business leader.*"

Chuck Corbin, Vice President, Strategy and
Business Development, BancTec, Inc.

"*Most business books leave you hanging somewhere between 'too theoretical' and 'too simplistic' and nothing ever gets applied.* Stick with It *is all about application, application, application—striking the right balance of explaining the why's and giving clear steps on how. You will not be left hanging.*"

John C. Bentley, Executive Vice President
Retirement Advisors of America

"*Stick with It* *is unusually clear and straightforward for books on this topic. The authors outline a simple, actionable blueprint for building a successful and profitable organization.*"

Dudley Hafner, Former CEO
American Heart Association, Inc.

"If you are looking for the keys to making your strategy come to life, you have found it in Stick with It. *The authors present an easy-to-follow blueprint for executing any strategy. They address the critical components of mastering the art of adherence—from focus to competence to passion. A must read for anyone responsible for delivering results!"*

Matt Krzysiak, CEO
National Motor Club

*"*Stick with It *provides a simple yet elegant blueprint for success for any organization. Despite the fact that we live in a rapidly changing, inter-connected, and always-on world, the keys to success in life and in business remain the same, namely, that clarity of purpose, a solid game plan, and, most important consistent daily execution always produces superior results.* Stick with It *should be required reading for every leader. I know it will be for ours."*

Dave Borden, CEO
Pharmaceuticals Strategies Group

"The beauty of Stick with It *is that it embodies the very principles it sets out to teach—focus and simplicity. Lee and Julie present strategies that will transform managers into leaders. It charts a clear course for personal accountability and challenges every individual to take the leap from where they currently are to what they can become!"*

Sharon Goldstein, Campus Operating Officer
Berkeley College Online

"For change to matter, it must endure. Lee and Julie lay out thought-provoking and relevant tools to make change, but also to create and sustain impact that really sticks."

Dean Carter, Chief HR Officer
Sears Holdings

"Stick with It *is a treasure chest of practical advice. A plan can be brilliant, but if you don't have the confidence in it to execute it with precision and consistency, you cannot succeed. Tenacity is critical to personal success in any area of life. This book is a powerful reminder of that basic truth."*

David L. Boren, President
University of Oklahoma

"Serving on boards and being a student of the 'pillars of wisdom' for the last 20 years has allowed me to see, hear, and read the work of great thought leaders—Lee and Julie Davis-Colan are among the elite. The Colans' discipline of simplicity with depth is compelling. Stick with It *is beautifully framed and sequenced. It presents a system of thinking and acting that, if followed, can be the basis of your personal and professional success."*

Jerry McNabb
McNabb Advisory
Advisor to Affluent Families and Their Businesses

"The authors of Stick with It *artfully make the point that adhering to your organizational plan is the key success determinant. This is another outstanding, actionable book by Colan for those of us seeking to optimize our organizations' effectiveness and success."*

Stephen L. Mansfield, PhD, FACHE
President and CEO
Methodist Health System

"Stick with It *captures in an exceptional way the challenges faced by leaders in maintaining a sharp focus on the execution of strategy, especially when facing the immense tactical pressures of day-to-day business."*

Raanan Horowitz, CEO
Elbit Systems of America

Stick with It

Other Books by Lee J. Colan

- *Engaging the Hearts and Minds of All Your Employees*
- *Leadership Matters: Daily Insights to Inspire Extraordinary Results*
- *Winners ALWAYS Quit* (with David Cottrell)
- *The Nature of Excellence* (with David Cottrell and Tom Fox)
- *7 Moments . . . That Define Excellent Leaders*
- *107 Ways to Stick to It*
- *Power Exchange: How to Boost Accountability and Performance in Today's Workforce*
- *INSPIRE! Connecting with Students to Make a Difference*
- *Orchestrating Attitude: Getting the Best from Yourself and Others*
- *Passionate Performance: Engaging Minds and Hearts to Conquer the Competition*
- *Sticking to It: The Art of Adherence*

Stick with It

Mastering the Art of Adherence

Lee J. Colan, PhD
and Julie Davis-Colan

New York Chicago San Francisco Lisbon London Madrid Mexico City
Milan New Delhi San Juan Seoul Singapore Sydney Toronto

1 2 3 4 5 6 7 8 9 0   DOC/DOC   1 9 8 7 6 5 4 3

ISBN 978-0-07-180253-6

MHID 0-07-180253-3

e-ISBN 978-0-07-180254-3

e-MHID 0-07-180254-1

Library of Congress Cataloging-in-Publication Data

Colan, Lee J. (Lee Joseph)
    Stick with it : mastering the art of adherence / by Lee Colan and Julie
Davis-Colan.
        pages cm
    Includes bibliographical references and index.
    ISBN-13: 978-0-07-180253-6 (alk. paper)
    ISBN-10: 0-07-180253-3 (alk. paper)
    1. Success in business. 2. Persistence. 3. Leadership. 4. Executive ability. I.
Davis-Colan, Julie. II. Title.
    HF5386.C7278 2013
    658.4'09--dc23   2012045754

McGraw-Hill books are available at special quantity discounts to use as
premiums and sales promotions or for use in corporate training programs.
To contact a representative, please e-mail us at bulksales@mcgraw-hill.com.

Contents

Acknowledgments

We want to thank all our clients, business partners, colleagues, and friends from whom we have learned a great deal. Your projects, conversations, creativity, and insights over the past 14 years have helped us refine and bring to life the concepts in this book. We thank God for bringing each of you into our lives. Our hope is that this book has as positive an impact on our readers as you have had on us.

Gratefully,

Lee J. Colan and Julie Davis-Colan
April 2013

Introduction:
Winning in Today's World

How do you win in today's world?

Is it having a distinct competitive advantage, such as exceptional talent, a cutting-edge product, or standout service? Perhaps it comes down to being able to anticipate market trends or fostering a culture of creativity and innovation. Or maybe the answer is having the best strategy. While all these factors are clearly important, none (nor all) guarantees success.

So, what is the answer? Sticking with your plan. The topic of executing your plans might not be currently trending on Twitter, but it is the key to success. You can be the best and have all the advantages, but to win, you must execute consistently. Plain and simple. It is not necessarily easy, but it is certainly simple.

In 2003, Lee wrote a rapid-read handbook on the topic of consistent execution titled *Sticking to It*. In the years since, the world has changed dramatically. Consider that in 2003 smartphones didn't exist and the iPod was only two years old. Facebook, Twitter, and YouTube had not yet launched, and LinkedIn was in its infancy. AOL was at its peak and virtually no one texted. Blockbuster and Lehman Brothers were the darlings of their respective industries. And few people had heard of an Illinois senator named Barack Obama.

A lot has changed in the last 10 years, but one thing hasn't: Sticking with it is still the biggest factor for winning in business and in life. Today, we face never-ending, rapid-fire change including constantly shifting priorities, sweeping advances in technology and communication, fluctuating markets, and heightened global competition. Let's face it. It's tough to stick with anything in this kind of environment. Yet this is precisely the reason why adhering to your strategy is so vitally important to long-term success.

Our mission has always been to provide our clients, readers, and audiences with clear thinking and practical tools to help them succeed in a "more, better, faster" world. We know your time is a precious and limited resource. That's why this book cuts through the information clutter and explains the *how* of sticking with it using a simple blueprint. Understanding why and how the highest performers consistently win will help you achieve breakthrough results and propel you ahead of your competition.

We have been privileged to collaborate with, advise, interview, and train more than 20,000 leaders on this topic. It has been an enriching opportunity for us to learn from leaders at every level, in organizations of all sizes, from fast-growing small businesses to Fortune 100s, and across all industries. Many of these organizations and leaders have applied the concepts in this book to win, and you will find their insights, advice, and real-world experiences throughout.

Achieving your goals is a primary business benefit of consistent execution. However, those who consistently execute their plans predictably realize these additional benefits, that combine to create a powerful and sustainable competitive advantage:

- Increased productivity and improved morale
- Improved accountability and follow-through
- Better results with fewer resources
- Elevated market position and employer brand

While each of us may have different goals and dreams, we all have one thing in common: We want to win! Whether you lead an entire organization, a small department, or just yourself, applying the action-

able steps found in *Stick with It* will guide you to victory.
So, get ready to win!

Look for the QR codes throughout the book to
download free tools that will help you stick with it.
www.theLgroup.com/StickwithIt

PART I

The **Art**
of
Adherence

1

The Knowing-Doing Gap

How many times have we been told that the formula for maintaining a healthy weight is to eat a balanced diet and exercise regularly? Although sophisticated marketers package this information in many creative ways, it's really quite simple: calories in equal calories out. If we know the formula, then why do so many of us still struggle to lose weight? The real secret to maintaining a healthy weight is not in knowing the formula, but in executing it. That is where our challenge seems to lie—in applying what we already know.

This same dynamic is magnified every year on January 1, when millions of us make New Year's resolutions. The beginning of a new year is a time to start fresh, to set new goals, and to make new plans for various areas of our lives. But we all know what happens. We slip back into our routine, and those resolutions fall by the wayside. A recent survey by FranklinCovey found that 35 percent of people break their resolutions by the end of January (many in less than a week) and that a mere 23 percent of New Year's resolutions are ever kept.[1]

It's not that our intentions are bad; quite the contrary. And it's not that we don't know how to tackle our resolutions. The problem is that most of us don't stick with it long enough to permanently change our behavior and get the results we want. (It takes at least 21 days of repeated action for a new behavior to become a habit.) **There is a knowing-doing gap—we know what to do, but fail to do it consistently.**

The same knowing-doing gap happens in business every day. Organizations develop brilliant strategies and are initially motivated to implement them. And yet many don't adhere to their strategies long enough to achieve the desired results. Most organizations understand how to develop a strategy, but many fail to successfully execute it. Consider the following findings:

- Ernst & Young found that a full 66 percent of corporate strategy are never executed.[2]
- Robert Kaplan and David Norton (*The Strategy-Focused Organization*) reveal that 90 percent of well-formulated strategies fail due to poor execution.[3]
- Deloitte identified top executives' single biggest hindrance to their companies' growth was "poor execution of strategy."[4]

Now consider that in a typical year about 15 percent of CEOs are removed from their posts.[5] Why? Of course, some have poor strategies. However, if we read between the lines of most corporate press releases, the most common reason CEOs lose their leadership positions is that they don't fully execute their strategies. In fact, according to highly regarded business consultant Ram Charan and *Fortune* columnist Geoffrey Colvin, 70 percent of CEO failures come not as result of poor strategy but of poor execution.[6] Chief executives are well aware of the challenges. According to a survey of 769 CEOs by The Conference Board, "excellence in execution" ranked as their number one business challenge.[7]

Lack of strategy execution is not isolated to the c-suite. Leaders at all levels and in every corner of the organization, from the production line to sales, experience challenges in executing their plans. For example, many organizations have formal quality processes in place, yet still deal with quality concerns. Chances are that frontline team members understand the quality control processes but don't consistently apply them. Safety is another area in which the knowing-doing gap is prevalent. Safety professionals know all too well the challenges of trying to get employees to follow safety procedures.

But perhaps nowhere in business is the knowing-doing gap more obvious than in sales. For many businesses, sales are a numbers game: a specified number of calls lead to a certain number of prospects that generate requests for proposals that ultimately yield a predictable number of sales. It's the classic sales funnel. Salespeople know the formula behind the funnel and are typically well trained in sales techniques. Those who execute consistently are high performers, the sales superstars. Those who consistently fail to execute, fail.

The consensus among strategy experts is that formulating strategy is relatively easy compared to executing it. But why is it so difficult for us to stick with our plan? What is at the root of this knowing-doing gap? In his book, *Making Strategy Work: Leading Effective Execution and Change*, Wharton School Management Professor Lawrence Hrebiniak proposes that execution is difficult primarily because:

- Leaders are trained to plan rather than to execute.

- Senior leadership tends to leave execution to lower-level leaders and team members and to review progress only periodically.

- Execution requires more people than strategy formulation. Developing strategy is typically done by relatively few people, whereas execution is a teamwide or businesswide endeavor.

- Execution requires more time than strategy formulation. Developing strategy is one action step; execution is a continuous, long-term process.[8]

Execution is simple in theory but difficult to put into practice. The great baseball player Yogi Berra was known as much for his witticisms as for his on-the-field performance. Berra had keen insight when he said, "In theory, there is no difference between theory and practice. In practice there is."

Filling the Knowing-Doing Gap

The greatest challenge for today's leaders is not a lack of innovative strategies but a lack of disciplined execution of these strategies. The game is won not by those who stand on the sidelines with a great plan in hand nor those who execute their plans when it is convenient or easy. Rather, the game is won by those who are committed to executing their plans day in and day out. Conceptually, this seems valid and logical, but does it hold true in real organizations run by real people? To answer that question, let's look at research based on real companies from all over the world that know how to execute and get results.

In 2012, *Fortune* magazine and Hay Group conducted a global survey to identify the world's most admired companies and to determine which best practices catapulted these companies to (or kept them at) the top of the list. The study looked at the Fortune 1000, the Global 500, and the top foreign companies operating in the United States. The four characteristics that distinguish the world's most admired companies are:

1. Strategic excellence
2. Structures and processes that sustain performance over time
3. Achieving success through people
4. Placing a high value on leadership and talent

The report concluded: "This doesn't just mean the World's Most Admired Companies are good at making plans (though they are). Where they shine is in their ability to make strategy happen, by aligning both their organizations and their people with key goals and objectives, by seeing things through. . . . Most companies devote a lot of attention to strategic planning. But the Most Admired Companies also put those strategies into practice."[9]

In other words, the world's most admired companies know how to stick with it. They may not have completely eliminated the knowing-doing gap, but they have certainly reduced it enough to create a significant competitive advantage.

Of course it's nice to be recognized as one of the world's most admired companies. However, bottom-line results are key indicators of an organization's health. So how do the top 50 world's most admired companies compare in that respect? Below is a comparison of total shareholder returns for these same companies versus the S&P 500.[10]

	Shareholder Returns For Top 50 World's Most Admired Companies	Shareholder Returns for S&P 500
Year of Study	22.6%	15.1%
Previous 3 Years	4.3%	(2.8%)
Previous 5 Years	8.3%	2.3%
Previous 10 Years	7.8%	1.4%

In every time period, the world's most admired companies outperformed not only the competition within their industries but also the market as a whole. And over a 10-year period, their returns were *five times* that of the S&P 500. These are pretty compelling differences. They are even more amazing when you consider the simplicity of the four differentiating characteristics: strategy, structure, people, and leadership. Could it really be that simple? Yes, it is. The difference between the world's most admired companies and the rest of the pack is that they do the basics exceptionally well and they execute their strategies masterfully.

These findings confirm that having a sound strategy is only one piece of a winning formula. Disciplined execution is the game-changer. How much of a game changer? A survey by the Economist Intelligence Unit (a sister organization of CFO.com) of 197 executives attempted to determine the value of filling the knowing-doing gap.

These senior executives predicted that if they were to stick with it and become "very effective" at strategy execution, they would likely improve operating profits by an average of 30 percent over two years.[11]

Bottom line: **Consistent execution consistently wins.**

Ideas are easy. It's the execution of ideas that really separates the sheep from the goats.

SUE GRAFTON, NOVELIST

2

What Is Adherence?

I n business and in life, the game is usually won by those who can consistently execute a well-thought-out strategy. In other words, winners stick with it—they practice adherence.

Adherence is the ability to consistently execute. Not coincidentally, the word "adherence" appears to have originated in the 1500s from the French word "adherer," which means "to stick to."[1] Adherence is the critical link between strategy (knowing) and results (doing). Therefore, it is the solution to the knowing-doing gap. Winning requires adherence because successful execution of your plan is not a one-time event but rather steady progress over an extended period of time.

No discussion about the concept of adherence would be complete without mentioning one man who likely knew more about adherence in his day than any other: George de Mestral. George was a Swiss engineer and part-time inventor. A simple incident in 1948 changed the course of his life and led to a common product that is still used all over the world.

While he was out hunting with his dog one day, George found that his pants and his dog's fur were covered with burdock burrs. He had such difficulty removing the burrs that he became intrigued with the little seeds' pods. Later when he was back home, he examined one under a microscope. George noticed that it was covered with hundreds of tiny "hooks" that allowed it to grab hold of strands of clothing or fur. Inspired by nature's ingenuity, he conceived the idea for a similar fastener based on the burr's design.[2]

After several years of trial and error and working with a weaver in France, George perfected the design for his "locking tape." He called his invention Velcro®, from the French words *velours* and *crochet* (meaning "velvet" and "hook"), and was awarded a patent for the world's first hook-and-loop fastener in 1955. George quit his job, established his own company, and obtained a $150,000 loan to market the concept. Velcro was officially introduced in 1960, but it was not an immediate commercial success. It took some time before people began to grasp its many applications. Eventually, it was adopted by industries as varied as aerospace and children's clothing, making de Mestral a multimillionaire many times over.

Today, Velcro is a household name. It is found in everything from sneakers and wallets to blood-pressure cuffs and toys. It was used on the space shuttle and helped hold a human heart together during the first artificial heart surgery.[3] It was even used as a piece of comedic genius in 1984 when late night talk show host David Letterman launched himself from a trampoline onto a Velcro wall while wearing a Velcro suit. He stuck.

It took George de Mestral 12 years from the day he first encountered those sticky burrs to the time he brought his locking tape idea to market and even longer for it to become a success. Not only did he tenaciously stick to his plan, but the product he planned and then executed literally stuck to him. So when you think of adherence, think of George de Mestral. Perhaps we should dub him "the father of adherence." He stuck with it long enough to create one of the stickiest materials we know.

The Adherence Equation

So how do you achieve adherence? How can you ensure that you will stick with your strategy long enough to win? Fortunately, adherence is a skill that can be learned. Based on the experiences of winning individuals, teams, and organizations, we have identified three components of adherence:

- **Focus** provides the clarity necessary to make decisions that support your most important goals. It results in a clearly defined pathway to success. A sharp focus answers the "what" question. *What* do you need to do to execute your strategy?

- **Competence** is used in the broadest sense of the term. It encompasses all the skills, systems, processes, and tools a team uses to achieve its goals. The result is the ability to commit to, measure, and hit your targets. Building competence answers the "how" question. *How* will you execute your strategy?

- **Passion** creates a sense of connectedness. It creates a connection between teammates, a connection to our human need for meaningful work, and a connection to each individual's sense of value and contribution. Igniting passion answers the "why" question, *Why* are you executing your strategy?

The relationship between these three components is best illustrated by a multiplication equation we call the adherence equation:

When you think about adherence this way, the critical role of each component becomes clear. From elementary school math we know that if any multiplier in an equation is 0, then the product is 0. For example, assume that each of the three components—focus, competence, and passion—are rated on a scale from 0 to 10, with 0 being the lowest and 10 being the highest. If any one of the three components is missing, (e.g., focus = 0), then there is no adherence:

Focus	x	Competence	x	Passion	=	Adherence
0	x	4	x	8	=	0

The three adherence components are interrelated, meaning that changes in one affect changes in the others, similar to the way the various systems of the human body affect one another. As you address one component of the equation—or conversely, as you ignore one—you will see direct implications in the other two. Consider what happens with a modest improvement in all three components:

Focus	x	Competence	x	Passion	=	Adherence
5	x	5	x	5	=	125
6	x	6	x	6	=	216

A modest improvement in each component produces a 73 percent increase in adherence (125 to 216). This underscores the compounding relationship among these components. Focus, competence, and passion are equally important and more powerful together.

This interrelationship creates a multiplier effect that can work for you (or against you if the components are not managed). Enhancing one component creates a multiplier effect on your adherence. As we discuss each of the three components, you will see the connections and notice that focus, competence, and passion are not three distinct and separate elements; rather, they are interconnected dynamics that influence and build upon each other.

The Art of Adherence

As we discuss at the beginning of this book, adherence is simple but not necessarily easy. It takes skill and creativity to continually nurture focus, competence, and passion with your team. This is why we call it the *art* of adherence.

The art of adherence is a lot like growing Indian Thorny bamboo, which is native to Asia. Like many bamboo species, when this particular seed is planted, it requires the right amount of watering, sunlight, care, and feeding. It takes up to two years of this kind of careful attention for the bamboo to build a strong root structure, which is not visible aboveground. However, once the sprout finally breaks through the earth, the Indian Thorny bamboo can grow up to 100 feet in a month! When you consistently sharpen focus, build competence, and ignite passion, you build a strong foundation for adherence. Initially, you may not see many tangible results. But rest assured that things are happening beyond your sight. Adherence is growing. Leaders and team members begin to stick with it, to execute their plans consistently. Your team builds momentum as it adheres to its plan and achieves small goals that lead to bigger goals. The required effort decreases over time as actions become habits. Momentum continues to build, resulting in a self-reinforcing cycle of achievement. Then, seemingly overnight, your results will multiply.

Mastering the art of adherence is a primary job of every leader at every level of the organization, and the adherence equation is designed to help you do just that. It offers a proven way for you to consistently execute your plan. Before we dive into the components of focus, competence, and passion, let's explore the relationship between adherence and strategy.

I think our lives are akin to the Chinese bamboo tree.
Sometimes we put forth effort, put forth effort, and put forth effort
and nothing seems to happen. But if you do the right things
long enough, you'll receive the rewards of your efforts.

CATHY TRUETT, FOUNDER
CHICK-FIL-A

3

The Role of Strategy

The quality of your strategy is certainly important in order for your team to win. However, it is not the primary factor in seizing victory. The primary factor in winning is adherence. Winning is achieved through adherence. **Winning depends less on a brilliant plan than on consistent actions.**

While it may at first seem counterintuitive, research shows that adherence is indeed more important than the quality of your plan. *Fortune* magazine and the Hay Group studied the issue of strategy execution. The researchers found that virtually all the companies in the study:

- Saw strategy as important
- Had detailed implementation plans
- Used strategy to help identify what to *stop* doing.[1]

All the companies seemed to talk the "planning and strategy talk." However, these factors were not what differentiated the companies in the study from those that made *Fortune's* Top Ten Most Admired list. The characteristics that were unique to the Top Ten Most Admired Companies and separated them from their industries peers were:

- Roles were clearly defined for executives, managers, and employees (focus).

- Leaders were held accountable—both personally and for their team (competence).
- Performance measurement was continuous and aligned with the strategy (competence).
- Business visions and purpose were communicated deep into the organization (passion).[2]

The researchers concluded that for the top 10 companies, strategy execution was not an exercise—it was the focus of everything they did: "Even in highly competitive and rapidly changing environments, most admired companies are distinguished by their success in executing against strategic plans."[3] In other words, they had strong adherence to their plans. These companies knew how to create a strategy; but more important, they achieved superior results because they knew how to stick with it.

What this tells us is that although a solid strategy is important, it only gets you in the game. Adherence to the strategy is what propels you into the winner's circle.

This is consistent with our observations over 25 years. Winning teams develop solid strategies (not always great ones) but they spend lots of time and energy to ensure they adhere to their strategies. One way to express this relationship between strategy and adherence is this:

$$\textbf{Strategy} \; + \; \underbrace{\textbf{Adherence}}_{\text{focus x competence x passion}} \; = \; \textbf{Level of Achievement}$$

This equation shows that strategy has only an additive impact on your achievement level, whereas adherence has a multiplier effect on achievement. For instance, if you have a mediocre strategy (say a 4 on a scale of 0 to 10) and your adherence is average (focus = 4, competence = 5, passion = 6), your achievement level would be:

$$4 \; + \; \underset{\underset{4 \times 5 \times 6}{\rule{0pt}{1.2em}\vert}}{120} \; = \; 124$$

Now assume that you really work on your strategy and make it great—say a 9 out of 10:

$$9 \; + \; \underset{\underset{4 \times 5 \times 6}{\rule{0pt}{1.2em}\vert}}{120} \; = \; 129$$

All your efforts to improve your strategy would result in a modest increase in achievement from 122 to 129.

But now let's say that you put that same effort into adhering to your original strategy (even though it was a mediocre one) instead of focusing on improving the strategy itself. Even if you slightly improve on every component of adherence by only 1 point (focus = 5, competence = 6, passion = 7), your achievement level gets a significant boost:

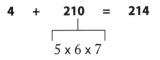

$$4 \; + \; \underset{\underset{5 \times 6 \times 7}{\rule{0pt}{1.2em}\vert}}{210} \; = \; 214$$

Because of the multiplier effect, this small improvement in each component of adherence results in a greater than 72 percent increase in achievement level (124 to 214), and this is with a mediocre strategy. Imagine what would happen if you improved your adherence even a little bit more.

This is why an average strategy with strong adherence tends to produce better results than a brilliant strategy with minimal adherence. So, **spend more effort on adherence than on tweaking your strategy.**

We certainly do not recommend blind adherence—sticking with a bad strategy at all costs. Winning organizations are keenly attuned to their marketplaces and are flexible enough to adjust strategies when necessary to address changing market conditions. However, leaders frequently tinker with strategy in ways that are often counterproductive. For example, new leaders typically feel pressure to "make their mark" on the team or organization. So a common reaction of these leaders is to shift strategic direction, regardless of whether the previous strategy was working.

We frequently find that when a strategy doesn't seem to be working, even seasoned leaders can be too quick to assume it's the strategy that is faulty rather than the execution. The opposite is usually true; the problem is execution. Constantly tinkering with strategy inhibits success by not allowing the original strategy to take root. On the other hand, leaders who stick with it see results.

You can observe this same principle in sports. Winning coaches tend to focus more on improving execution than on shifting strategy in reaction to a bad play, a loss, or a slump. In 2011, the NBA's Dallas Mavericks were a middle-of-the-pack playoff team (which is not saying much since more than half the teams make the playoffs). There were good odds that they would get knocked out in the first round of the playoffs. That prospect did not faze Mavericks coach Rick Carlisle. He stuck with his simple strategy of good passing, hustle, and team-oriented basketball, even against faster, stronger, more athletic teams. He continued to hone his team's ability to execute its game plan. As a result, the Mavericks were able to beat perennial powerhouses like the Los Angeles Lakers. We ultimately enjoyed watching our hometown team win the NBA championship by out-executing a Miami Heat team that had more youth, speed, and talent.

The ultimate competitive advantage, organizationally or personally—and even in sports—is being the very best at adhering to your strategy. If you do not adhere to your plan—even the very best plan—it is like having a great blueprint for a new house but never building it. It's just a plan, so don't start inviting friends over for the housewarming party yet. If you want to win, a good plan is necessary but not sufficient. You also have to stick with it to make your plan a reality.

Success doesn't necessarily come from breakthrough innovation but from flawless execution. A great strategy alone won't win a game or a battle; the win comes from basic blocking and tackling.

NAVEEN JAIN, BUSINESS
EXECUTIVE AND ENTREPRENEUR

4

Start with Strategy

While the key factor in winning is the ability to stick with your plan, it makes sense that you start with the best plan possible. Our experiences working with clients on strategic planning and execution indicate a direct correlation between the simplicity of a plan and the chances of adhering to it. A theme we hear over and over again is, "Give us three steps, and we will knock 'em out. Give us a three-ring binder, and it will sit on the shelf."

It is important to start with a simple, clear, and well-thought-out plan, whether you are developing a corporate strategic plan or setting your department's strategy. Why stack the odds against yourself with an overly complex or unclear plan? Our goal is to have clients articulate their plans in a just few pages. **If you are going to work on a plan, your plan should work for you.**

Management journals, books, and articles are filled with countless approaches to strategic planning. The definitions for the various components of a strategic plan can be debated endlessly—a vision versus a mission, initiatives versus tactics, goals versus objectives. So rather than use valuable client time debating definitions or working through a complex planning process, we cut through the clutter by answering six simple questions about your business or team (depending on your level in the organization). Think of these questions as the "Cliffs-Notes" version of planning. Develop clear answers to these questions, and you'll be off to a strong start. Don't be deceived by the simplicity of the questions. They require deep thought, good supporting data, and honest discussion in order to articulate concise answers. And remember, the questions apply to leaders of organizations, regional offices, departments, or small teams.

Six Simple Questions for a Winning Plan

Every leader should answer the following six questions for his or her function.

1. Why do we exist?

What promises are you making to customers? Which wants, needs, desires, pains, or problems do your products or services solve? The answer to this question should rarely change since it reflects the core of your existence. Keep your answer real and relevant because people can commit only to what they understand, and your leaders must be able to own and live the answer. And keep it simple. Anything more than a sentence might be too long to remember and too long for employees to really connect with.

Consider how your function or organization makes life better for others. Your answer should stir the emotions. It should not be a project goal (too time-restricted), financial target (not emotionally compelling), or a specific strategy (too narrow). People don't get emotionally charged about a "10 percent net profit," a "20 percent return on investment" or a "30 percent increase in market share." Your answer to this question should give your employees a reason to be excited about getting up and going to work every day, a reason to get excited about Monday mornings.

Your answer should also guide your team members in making daily decisions that support the core reason for your function's existence. One of the most powerful psychological human needs is the need for meaning or significance. We all want to contribute to something bigger than ourselves. When it comes to your plan, meaning precedes motivation. Give your team a connection to something meaningful, and they will provide discretionary effort.

Here is how a few winning organizations and teams have answered the "why do we exist" question (but don't be restricted by their structure or wording):

- **Google:** To organize the world's information and make it universally accessible and useful.

- **Bristol-Myers Squibb:** To discover, develop, and deliver innovative medicines that help patients prevail over serious diseases.

- **Coca-Cola:** To refresh the world, to inspire moments of optimism and happiness, to create value and make a difference.

- **National Motor Club:** To provide peace of mind and convenience for our traveling public.

- **Customer call center:** To brighten the day of each and every caller.

- **Information technology department:** To improve personal productivity.

- **Purchasing department:** To ensure that all company products are made with the best raw materials available.

Your team's purpose may not be apparent at first glance. For example, DW Distribution is a regional building products distributor in its third generation of family leadership. Its leaders experienced a common challenge when answering this question, "Why do we exist?" Like many companies, it was easy for the leaders to describe *what* they do instead of *why* they do it. Their initial response to this question was, "We move quality building products from point A to point B on time." While, in fact, this is what the company does, there was also a deeper "why." Since many of its products were used for new home construction, the ultimate answer was, "We distribute building products that help the American dream come true." Now, that's a purpose worth working for! If you have a clear, brief description of what you do, consider adding to the end of that statement the words, "so that" or "in order to." You will find that it makes for a much more meaningful and emotionally compelling answer because it answers why your function exists.

2. Where are we going?

The answer to this question should be a forward-looking statement that inspires your entire team, from customer-facing operations to back-office support. It should connect today's tasks to tomorrow's promise. The answer may change over time to drive constant learning and innovation.

Fossil is a worldwide watchmaker and also one of the fastest-growing lifestyle brands with its line of American vintage watches, accessories, clothing, and shoes. Jennifer Pritchard, president of retail for Fossil, has led its retail growth to 418 stores worldwide with a vision of being a distinctive lifestyle brand. Pritchard has been a client of ours for several years and shared her perspective on this question, "Where are we going?": "If you don't invest the time to know where you want to go, you will never be in a position to get there. It is in the development of your vision and strategy that you take the first real step toward making it a reality. Once you have your 'where' you can invest in the 'how'."[1]

Here are some other examples of answers to the question, "Where are we going?" Note that some of the examples are from the same companies and teams for which we gave examples to question 1:

- **Zappos:** One day, 30 percent of all retail transactions in the United States will be online. People will buy from the company with the best service and the best selection. Zappos.com will be that online store.
- **Nike:** To be the number one athletic goods company in the world.
- **DuPont:** To be the world's most dynamic science company, creating sustainable solutions essential to better, safer, and healthier lives for people everywhere.

- **National Motor Club:** To become the recognized number 1 quality service provider benefiting our customers and members.

- **Customer call center:** To always be in the industry's top 10 percent in response time and caller satisfaction.

- **Information technology department:** To consistently deliver 99 percent uptime for all business-critical systems.

- **Purchasing department:** To reduce our company's carbon footprint by 50 percent in the next five years.

3. How will we conduct ourselves?

Your answer to this question should reflect your values. It will influence how you design your people systems (e.g., selection, training, promotion, rewards) and your work systems (e.g., meeting ground rules, response expectations, decision making, quality control, collaboration, innovation). Consider these value pillars as you formulate your answer: customer, team, individual, and excellence. Think about the very few values you hold as core, as nonnegotiable. Avoid the typical, long laundry list of values and instead target three to five core values at most. For example, one of *Fortune's* most admired companies, Marriott, boils its values down to: put people first, pursue excellence, embrace change, act with integrity, and serve the world. We elaborate more on values in Chapter 18, "Value Your Values."

4. What will we do?

Strategies generally revolve around customers/markets, people/organizations, products/services, systems/technology, and distribution/sales channels. The answer to this question should address how your team will compete in the marketplace or service other departments (if you lead an internal service function). Consider what you will specifically do (and not do), who you will serve (and not serve), and how you will differentiate yourself. Will you enter new markets, roll out new products, leverage a new technology, consolidate operations, use a new marketing approach, build upon your supply chain, become more operationally efficient?

It is far better to limit yourself to a few strategies and stick with them than to formulate so many strategies that you can't fully execute them. Try to identify no more than three strategies to execute.

5. How will we measure success?

Measures of success tell you in quantifiable ways if you are making progress in executing your plan and, ultimately, if you have fully implemented it. The nature of your strategies will dictate what makes sense to measure: sales, profits per employee, expenses as a percent of sales, employee engagement level, return on equity, market share, customer satisfaction, year-over-year growth, and so on. We address the importance of measurement in Chapter 13, "Balance Your View."

6. What improvements or changes must we make?

Rarely does a solid strategy enable your team to proceed with business as usual—it should trigger some changes in order to take your performance to the next level. Your answer to this question should describe just a few key initiatives to support each strategy that you outlined in question 4. Let's assume that one of your strategies is to add services to support your product offerings in order to deepen customer loyalty. Key initiatives might include identifying those services customers perceive as most valuable to their product purchase and testing initial service offerings in key markets to measure customer and revenue impact.

The Simple Six in Action

Now that you've seen the questions, let's take a look at how a worldwide manufacturer of golf clubs might answer the simple six questions to develop a strategy:

1. **Why do we exist?** To bring confidence and winning strokes to golfers across the globe.
2. **Where are we going?** We will be a trusted club in the golf bag of 75 percent of the world's ranked professional golfers.

3. How will we conduct ourselves?

- Innovate in all we do—the big ideas and the little ideas.
- Respect our teammates and the profession we serve.
- Pour our hearts into our work. Every club is a reflection of us.

4. What will we do?

- Penetrate new markets.
- Boost brand exposure.
- Drive organizational efficiency.

5. How will we measure our success?

- Penetrate new markets
  - Increase sales from $5 million to $10 million in China and Japan.
  - Increase sales by 15 percent in the European market.
- Boost brand exposure
  - Achieve number 1 or 2 ranking in all professional player surveys of best brand of clubs.
  - Triple the number of brand impressions in Asian markets by year-end.
- Drive organizational efficiency
  - Reduce manufacturing waste by 10 percent by year-end and by 20 percent over three years.
  - Reduce expenses as a percent of sales by 5 percent by year-end and by 15 percent over three years.
  - Improve average employee engagement score to 4.5 by year-end and to 4.8 (top 1 percent in industry) in three years.

6. What improvements or changes must we make?

- Penetrate new markets

- Hire new sales leaders for Asia and Europe.
- Double pipeline of player endorsements in Asia and Europe by year-end.

- Boost brand exposure
  - Sign three new sponsorship deals with top 100 ranked players by year-end.
  - Double the number of tournaments for which we are a primary sponsor.
  - Sponsor 10 junior golfers' clinics in each geography.
- Drive organizational efficiency
  - Train all employees on innovation techniques.
  - Review lowest-performing products.
  - Implement passionate performance engagement model to drive employee engagement.

Six Simple Questions Template
www.theLgroup.com/StickwithIt

Answering these questions (and making corresponding budget adjustments) will get you started with a solid plan you can adhere to. However, your adherence to the plan will suffer unless all team members clearly understand the answers, so we discuss ways to keep your answers to the six simple questions visible in your organization in Chapter 9, "Keep It Visible."

Finally, keep in mind that just as we are devoting only one chapter to strategy development and the balance of the book on adhering to that strategy. **Winning leaders spend less time on strategy and more on adherence.**

In real life, strategy is actually very straightforward.
You pick a general direction and implement like hell.

JACK WELCH, FORMER CEO,
GENERAL ELECTRIC

5

Personal Adherence

dherence is just as challenging for us individually as it is professionally. We already know that few of us stick with our New
Year's resolutions, and we also have trouble sticking with other
plans we make throughout the year. For example, of those of us who
start a workout routine, about half will quit. Interestingly, the exercise dropout rate is nearly the same as it was 20 years ago despite the
growth of the fitness industry.[1]

Likewise, executing our plans is just as important in our personal
lives as it is in our professional lives, perhaps even more so. Our personal plans affect our personal well-being, and our well-being impacts
virtually every aspect of our lives. Furthermore, our personal lives and
professional lives are intertwined. We tend to bring our work home
with us and we also tend to take our personal challenges and successes
to work.

Personal adherence is crucial for another reason: adherence, like
most aspects of leadership, works inside out, meaning that we must
start with ourselves. **We win from within.** Effective team performance
begins with effective personal performance, and team adherence begins with personal adherence. We must lead from the inside out—
making personal changes and improvements before we can credibly
ask our teams to do the same. The power of role modeling is true in
every aspect of our lives. Children mimic their parents' values, behaviors, and habits. It has been and always will be that way. This deeply

rooted human behavior of modeling those who lead us is as powerful in the work setting as it is in the home.

In our work with clients, we occasionally see leaders take an outside-in approach—they attempt to change their teams before changing themselves. For example, they tell their teams to be more focused, and yet they are not focused as leaders. Although an outside-in approach can produce short-term results, it will rarely, if ever, produce long-term, sustained change. In fact, most organizational change efforts fail within the first 18 months for exactly this reason—leaders take an outside-in approach to change. This yields compliance rather than commitment from their teams. And behavior change for the sake of compliance is rarely "owned" as deeply as we need in order to sustain high performance.

We must first master self-leadership before we can expect to effectively lead others. Think of self-leadership like this: Every action you take is like a pebble tossed into a quiet pond. Your actions affect others' actions, which create a ripple effect of reactions. **There are no neutral actions;** everything we do has a positive or negative impact of some sort. This is especially true for leaders. Your team members are watching everything you do. Your actions and attitudes have a direct effect on their actions and attitudes. Whether or not your team members have ever said the words out loud, their mantra is, "If you can't lead yourself, then don't lead me." Winning leaders start with themselves, and they don't have to assert their leadership because others naturally want to follow them.

If you want your team to stick with it, start with yourself. The good news is that the art of adherence is the same regardless of the application—personal or professional. There is nothing mysterious about the way high-performing individuals achieve their results. They don't follow fads or trends. They execute the basics, day in and day out, whether it is how they eat, exercise, learn, invest, serve, read, listen, prepare, or work. The critical difference between winners and the rest is their ability to stick with it.

If you want high and sustained results on the outside, remember that it starts on the inside. Master the art of adherence in your own life first. To help you do that, we've included a chapter on personal adherence for each component of the adherence equation. These chapters include examples of people who demonstrate excellent personal adherence, along with practical actions you can take to sharpen your personal focus, build your personal competence, and ignite your personal passion.

So start preparing for victory with the art of adherence. The rest of this book reveals the adherence accelerators and will equip you with tools you need to win.

Self-leadership is the ability to get yourself to do what needs to be done, when it needs to be done, whether you feel like it or not, and still do it well.

JIM CATHCART, MOTIVATION EXPERT AND AUTHOR

PART II

Focus

Focus X (Competence) X (Passion) = **ADHERENCE**

We have an 18-year family ritual of going to the circus when Ringling Bros. and Barnum & Bailey comes to town. We have seen some amazing acts in 18 different shows—if it can be balanced, juggled, jumped over, walked on, ridden, or shot out of a cannon, whether by human or animal, we've seen it. But one act in particular always fascinates us: the lion tamer—one courageous person locked in a cage with six or seven beasts that can eat the tamer for lunch if they choose.

The lion tamer typically uses three tools to control his fierce companions prowling around the cage: a whip, a stool, and a handful of tasty snacks. But which of these tools is most valuable to the tamer? You might think it's the whip, but it's not. It's the stool. When the lion tamer lifts the stool to face his snarling friends, the lions see all four stool legs and don't know which one to focus on. As a result, the lions stand frozen, enabling the tamer to keep them at bay.

Unfortunately, the same can happen to us when we try to focus on too many things at once—we are unable to take action on any of them. Lack of focus significantly impacts our ability to adhere to our plan.

In our dealings over the past 25 years with leaders at all levels across virtually every industry, focus is always at the top of their list of adherence challenges. Imagine that. Today, after 25 years of unprecedented globalization, hypercompetition, and technology advancement, the same primary challenge exists for leaders—keeping teams focused amidst the whirlwind of constant change. We recently saw a cynical but true poster that read, "When the winds of change blow hard enough, even the most trivial of objects can become deadly projectiles." Can you relate? In the midst of change, even the smallest issue can become a serious distraction.

Today's business environment offers a plethora of focus challenges, but once we find a way to sharpen our focus, we can clearly see the benefits. To illustrate the power of focus, consider two sources of energy: the sun and a laser. The sun is a powerful source of energy. It showers the Earth with billions of kilowatts of energy every hour. The sun is 12 million degrees at the core and 3 million degrees at the surface. Yet, with a hat and sunscreen, you can minimize most of the negative effects of exposure to this megasource of energy. On the other hand, a laser is a relatively weak source of energy. A laser takes just a few watts of energy and focuses them in a concentrated stream of light. But with a laser, you can drill a hole in a diamond or remove certain forms of cancer cells. That's the power of focus! A laser gives off less energy yet produces very efficient results because its energy is very focused.

The same principle applies to individual and team performance. If you are doing a little bit of everything, your team will be like the sun—lots of activity (energy) but diffused impact. However, when you concentrate your team's focus on your plan, you become laserlike, achieving more with less effort.

So if a clear focus is so powerful, why do leaders continue to struggle with diffused efforts toward achieving their plans? Focus is one of those concepts that is easy to talk about yet difficult to apply, especially in today's competitive, change-intensive, opportunity-rich, information-loaded business world. With so many distractions, it is hard to stay focused on your plan. The real-time nature of communication and information makes everything feel urgent even though certain things might not be important. While distractions themselves might not hinder your success, the energy they steal from you and your team can quickly derail your efforts.

The good news is that you have more control over your team's focus than you might think. Focus serves as a filter for allocating resources—time, attention, people, capital—toward your plan. Focus helps you make the crucial decisions about what you will commit your resources to, and just as importantly, what you will not commit them to. Focus also answers the "what" question—what do you need to do to execute your strategy? When you clearly and simply answer that question, your team will be honed in on your plan with laserlike precision.

Winning leaders use four adherence accelerators to sharpen their teams' focus. They:

1. Cut through complexity to keep things simple.
2. Have absolute clarity about the one thing that is most important.
3. Know when to say no to activities that diffuse their focus.
4. Keep their plans and critical goals visible for all to see.

We look at each of these adherence accelerators in more detail in the next four chapters.

If you don't know where you are going,
you will probably end up somewhere else.

LAURENCE JOHNSTON PETER,
AUTHOR OF *THE PETER PRINCIPLE*

6

Keep It Simple

Keeping things simple helps your team stay focused. This seems like it should be easy enough, but as billionaire investor Warren Buffett says, "There seems to be some perverse human characteristic that likes to make easy things difficult."[1] We do, in fact, live in a complex world of advancing technology, global competition, brand abundance, unprecedented variety of sales and distribution channels, and blossoming new work arrangements and organizational structures. Despite all this we argue that over the past 25 years, the core principles of running an enterprise and adhering to a plan remain unchanged. Business gurus like Peter Drucker and Tom Peters might even say that the basics of business haven't changed in 50 years.

Discerning leaders look beyond timely complexity to find timeless simplicity. They recognize simplicity as a winning strategy. For example, a study of 39 midsized German companies found that only one characteristic differentiated the high-performing companies from the less successful ones—simplicity. High performers sold fewer products, had fewer customers, and worked with fewer suppliers than other companies in the same industry that were less profitable. This study, detailed in the book *Simplicity Wins* by a team of McKinsey & Company consultants, found that simple, focused operations were more profitable.[2]

So how do you decrease complexity in an ever-more complex business environment? Let's look at two ways to simplify.

Think in Threes

In a complex world, we need straightforward methods to help us simplify; complicated processes only create more complexity and compound the problem. Thinking in threes is a technique we have been using for years. It is a powerful way to simplify organizational thinking. As a by-product, it also forces prioritization and focus, and the resulting clarity trickles down into the organization. For example, we routinely ask clients to reduce their strategies from perhaps six to three, or to consolidate their values from twelve to three, or to select the three most important business metrics from their laundry list of twenty. No doubt, it's a struggle. But we have successfully used this technique countless times to help clients simplify their values, measures, strategies, action plans, and message points.

Truth be told, ending up with precisely three items is less important than the clarity this process creates. For instance, when we encouraged a client to identify just three core values instead of its list of twelve (that no one could remember let alone apply), the client settled on four values. It wasn't necessary to eliminate one more to get down to three values. The benefit was realized—clear articulation of the core values that virtually everyone in the organization now remembers and lives by.

Thinking in threes forces us to create simple, memorable, focused frameworks for our plans, our values, and our metrics.

Identify Your 80/20

Another powerful way to keep things simple is to apply the 80/20 principle. It quickly reveals the simplicity in your environment. The 80/20 principle is pervasive in our world:

- 80 percent of traffic jams occur on 20 percent of roads.
- 80 percent of beer is consumed by 20 percent of consumers.
- 80 percent of the time we wear 20 percent of our wardrobe options.

The 80/20 principle is also alive and well in business:

- 80 percent of profits come from 20 percent of products or services.
- 80 percent of service problems are generated by 20 percent of causes.
- 80 percent of sales are generated by 20 percent of salespeople.

If the 80/20 principle exists in your business, this means the most productive one-fifth of your business is 16 times more productive than the remaining four-fifths. This can seem counterintuitive so we have illustrated how it works:

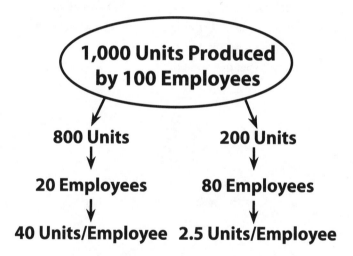

The same principle applies to your customers, products, regions, and employees. For example, we worked with a high-growth technology business during the last economic downturn. The CEO knew that he had to make some tough decisions that would require deep head-count reductions, including 70 percent of his sales team. You can imagine his sense of impending doom with the prospects of a skeleton sales force. To allay his anxiety, we suggested a quick-and-dirty 80/20 analysis of the company's sales by salesperson. Our client was astounded and relieved to find that 90 percent of sales were generated by 30 percent of the salespeople. So although he had to cut 70 percent of his sales force, he retained 90 percent of sales with the remaining 30 percent of the sales team.

Do you know who or what your best 20 percent are—your "vital few"? Don't rely only on your instincts to identify them—use data to determine where the 80/20 principle is in your organization. Look at your locations, products, prospecting channels, services, and people to find the vital few that drive the majority of your productivity, profitability, new business leads, waste, customer complaints, or downtime. You may find that only two types of errors cause 80 percent of the rework or that only a few products produce 90 percent of your sales or customer complaints. You may also discover that a small number of the services you provide generate the largest amount of activity for your team or that a particular department causes 80 percent of the conflict on which your team spends its energy.

80/20 Principle Worksheet
www.theLgroup.com/StickwithIt

Leveraging the 80/20 principle is a great way to decrease complexity in your business. It allows you to simplify by focusing on those elements that have the biggest impact on your plan (vital few) and not get distracted by all the other elements that have less impact (trivial many). Once you have identified the elements that make up your 20 percent, learn from them by determining which characteristics make them successful. Then you can work to enhance those characteristics even more and/or use those characteristics as best practices to improve in other areas.

While your trivial many might dilute your focus, by no means are we suggesting you eliminate them. Often there are good reasons they exist, such as serving as a loss leader, testing new products or geographies, or complementing your vital few so that you can offer customers a more complete solution. However, our clients frequently find that their trivial many are often "leftovers" from the past or sacred cows that no one has been willing to eliminate. As you focus on your vital few, you will naturally begin a gradual shedding of your trivial many. For example, you could consider automating, streamlining, or outsourcing areas that are not core to your team's operation. The point is to be intentional about where and how you apply your focus. Winning teams conduct periodic 80/20 analyses to learn from the vital few and to shed the trivial many as appropriate.

Complexity is the enemy of focus and adherence. Keeping things simple in your business makes it easier to stick with your plan. Yet even with a simple model or framework, we still need to sharpen our focus further. We explore how you can do that in the next chapter by identifying your "one thing."

Chapter At-a-Glance

- **Keep it simple**
  - Think in threes to simplify strategies, metrics, messages, and actions.

  - Apply the 80/20 principle to focus on the 20 percent that are your vital few.

Genius is the ability to reduce the complicated to the simple.

C. W. CERAM, AUTHOR

7

Identify Your "One Thing"

D o you remember the movie *City Slickers*? In the movie, a group of friends from the city takes a "vacation" at a dude ranch. Curly, played by Jack Palance, is a hard, crusty old cowboy full of wisdom. He gives some great advice to Mitch, played by Billy Crystal, who is facing some midlife questions. Here is the scene:

Curly: You all come out here about the same age. Same problems. Spend 50 weeks a year getting knots in your rope—then you think two weeks up here will untie them for you. None of you get it. Do you know what the secret of life is?

Mitch: No, what?

Curly: This. (Holds up his index finger.)

Mitch: Your finger?

Curly: One thing. Just one thing. You stick to that, and everything else don't mean [anything].

Great scene. Great advice. For the purposes of sharpening focus, **your "one thing" is the one activity that most directly helps you execute your plan.** It's the most vital of your vital few activities. Each day, each week, each month, each quarter, and each year, there is just one thing that is most vital for you to do in order to execute your plan.

Unitasking

This singular focus might seem counterintuitive in today's do-more world. In fact, in many organizations (and homes), juggling multiple priorities has become a way of life. After all, why work on just one thing when technology enables us to do many things at once? But contrary to popular belief, studies have repeatedly proven that multitasking is less efficient and less productive. Much of what we call multitasking is actually task switching—quickly moving from one task to another to another. Either way, the results are the same: Productivity decreases by as much as 40 percent.[1] As our productivity declines, so does quality. The reality is that most of us can do only one or two tasks at a time with excellence. When we gravitate from three to four things, our performance becomes mediocre. When we push the limits and try to focus on five or more tasks at a time, we tend to produce poor-quality work.

Every goal or activity cannot have equal priority. Treating everything with equal priority only diffuses focus and decreases adherence. That's why many experts agree with cowboy Curly's wisdom of focusing on just one thing. Sherry Turkle, MIT professor and founder of the MIT Initiative on Technology and the Self, argues that society needs to move away from multitasking in favor of unitasking. Speaking at the *The Economist's* Human Potential Summit, Turkle said, "The challenge for corporations and individuals in the years ahead is to put a new value on unitasking. We need to make it okay to do one thing at a time. We need to retrain ourselves to be unitaskers."[2]

Don't be tempted to think that you can keep piling on the initiatives and still maintain your team's focus. Resist the urge to multitask yourself or your team. Instead, create a habit of unitasking—focusing on the one thing that is most vital for that day, week, month, and so on.

Identifying your one thing forces a laserlike focus on the highest-impact activities and ensures that your team acts in alignment with the broader plan. The megaconnected, real-time, highly distracted world we live in makes identifying your one thing especially challenging.

There are more real-time decisions to make in today's business environment than ever before. It's all too easy to be ruled by the tyranny of the urgent—to feel compelled to handle urgent tasks (e-mails, phone calls, interruptions, the trivial many) while the truly important tasks that help us execute our plan get rolled over to the next day, and then the next week, and then the next month.

The most important decision is to decide what is most important. We must be discerning in order to identify the single most important thing to work on in any given moment. Start with yourself and ask, "What is most important thing I can do right now to execute our plan?" Identify the most important goal for the organization. That should drive your department's goal, which in turn should dictate your goal. Therefore, your one thing (most important activity) should support your team's top priority. Your team's priority should support your department's goal, and so on all the way up the enterprise, so that there is organizational alignment.

We must have laserlike clarity about our individual one thing and our team's one thing. If we are more like the sun—scattered in our clarity and focus—our team's efforts will also be scattered. This is the law of diffusion. There is a natural and predictable decrease in clarity as information and priorities filter down through an organization. The law of diffusion means that if a leader is crystal clear about the team's one thing (say a 9 on a clarity scale of 10), then even in the best of situations, clarity about the team's one thing on the front lines will be a 7 or an 8. If a leader is not very clear about the one thing (perhaps a 5 or 6), then where the rubber meets the road—at the front lines of customer interaction or on the production floor—people will have clarity of only 3 or 4, and that's not a winning formula.

Align Your One Thing

To counteract the law of diffusion, make certain your team members clearly understand their one thing, thus always ensuring that they directly connect to the organization's top priority. Use your team meetings to maintain focus on your most important tasks. Rather than following a traditional "around the table" report format, ask your team members what their one thing is for the day or week. It might be the most clarifying question you ask. In Chapter 9, "Keep It Visible," we discuss other ways to increase clarity and keep your one thing in front of your team.

UCLA Health System president, David Feinberg, keeps his one thing crystal clear and aligned throughout his organization. UCLA Health System is one of the most well-respected healthcare systems in the United States. It has 4 hospitals and 150 clinics, approximately 7,500 personnel and volunteers, and over 1.5 million patients served annually. More than 120 of its physicians were cited in a recent "best doctors in America" poll. But it was not always that way. While there are several factors that contributed to UCLA's assent to the top echelon of health systems, the key has been Feinberg's singular focus. The system's one thing, from top to bottom, is that the next patient receives great care—compassionate and quality care. Feinberg ensures that the one thing is constantly communicated and rigorously measured at all levels of the organization. Every team member's one thing is aligned from a frontline function all the way up to the enterprise level. Of course, this translates into different tasks depending on the individual's level and function, but all actions support the one thing of providing great care to the next patient.[3]

We recently experienced firsthand an example of alignment between a company's one thing and the actions of its frontline employees. It occurred on a Southwest Airlines flight. Southwest's one thing is customer service, and if you have ever flown on Southwest, you know that the spirit of service is palpable. But what we experienced was extraordinary. It was a short, 45-minute flight from Houston to Dallas, so the beverage service had to be handled quickly. We were busy discussing ideas for this book when we heard a commanding voice that didn't sound like the flight attendant asking if we wanted peanuts or pretzels. We looked up, and to our surprise, it was a uniformed captain (he was not one of the pilots flying the plane; he was en route to his assigned flight). The captain explained that the flight attendants had already handled many flights that day, so he thought he would pitch in. It was the perfect alignment of an organization's one thing, in this case customer service, from the executive suite to the aisle seat. That kind of alignment is a key factor behind Southwest Airlines' record of 39 consecutive years of profitability.

As a leader, your primary responsibility to your team, your organization, and your shareholders is to execute your plan. When you are clear about what is most important, like Feinberg is with his team, you will know the one thing you have to get done. If you get 99 percent of your job done but fail to complete the most important thing, then you will fail. But if you achieve only your one thing, you will succeed. Your one thing is today's stepping stone to tomorrow's victory.

Chapter At-a-Glance

- **Identify your one thing**
  - Decide what is most important—the one activity that most directly helps you execute your plan.
  - Align your one thing with the organization's most important priority.
  - Ask your team, "What is the most valuable thing you can do right now?"

Be like a postage stamp.
Stick to one thing until you get there.

Josh Billings, Humorist

8

Know When to Say No

Winning teams are both clear and passionate about their one thing. This powerful combination creates leadership courage, and this enables leaders to make difficult decisions for their teams such as swiftly channeling resources away from noncritical areas. Having the conviction to say no when necessary is a key differentiator between those who adhere to their plans and those who don't. Winners say no at two distinct levels: strategy and tactics.

Strategically, winning organizations follow the same principle advocated by management guru Peter Drucker who said, "If you want to grow your business, before you decide where and how to grow, the first thing you need to do is stop doing what's not working and get rid of the outgrown, the obsolete, and the unproductive. As a leader, you must have the courage to:

- Abandon projects that fail to deliver results;
- Abandon products and services that will fail to increase future profits;
- Abandon people that fail to make worthwhile contributions to the company."[1]

Pharmacy giant Walgreens did precisely that. Now one of two dominant players in the pharmacy market, Walgreens had to say no in order to get where it is today. At one point, Walgreens owned over 500 restaurants. Deciding that its future was in convenience drugstores, it made the commitment to be out of the restaurant business in five years. Leaders courageously stuck to their decision, which required saying no many times in order to ensure a redirection of resources back to their core business. The strategy worked. Saying no helped Walgreens become an industry leader with more than 8,000 locations.

When considering which strategic initiatives you need to say no to, start with an 80/20 analysis. That alone may shed light on strategies that are not adding value to your business. Then, ask your team this question: "If we were not involved in this strategy already, would we choose to pursue it today?" If your answer is no, then seriously consider abandoning it. Of course, we realize that in practice it's not that straightforward. But one has to seriously question the value of continuing with a strategy that does not contribute (it is one of the trivial many) and that you would not pursue today if you were presented with the same opportunity.

In today's market, there are often so many strategic opportunities to pursue that it can be difficult to say no. That's why we help leaders say no by creating a series of decision hurdles for evaluating new opportunities. Defining a set of hurdles helps efficient use of resources as you consider new opportunities. Think of each new opportunity as a hurdler. The opportunity must jump over key hurdles before you invest more time and energy analyzing it. For example, if an acquisition opportunity presents itself, the first hurdle might be, "Does it fit into our long-term strategy?" If the answer is no, then no more time needs to be spent on that decision. You just say no to the opportunity and move on. However, if the answer to the first hurdle is yes, the next hurdle might be, "Do the target company's products/services improve our market position (e.g., adjacent products or markets)?" Each subsequent hurdle gets more specific as the opportunity proceeds down the track. We suggest developing a set of three decision hurdles. That way, you can quickly and methodically consider opportunities with respect to these hurdles while still keeping focused on running your business. If an opportunity makes it over all the hurdles and to the finish line, you know you have a winner.

Saying no is just as important at the tactical level as it is at the strategic level. For example, perhaps you spend an hour or two each week reviewing reports. After stepping back and analyzing your time, you realize that you are not making key decisions based on those reports or that the reports are not helping you execute your plan. It's time either to change the content of the report so that it does support your plan or to say no to the reports and use the reviewing time for higher-impact activities.

If you find yourself saying, "That was a waste of my time," "How is this adding value to my team?" or "What decision is this helping me make?" this is a sign that you need to say no. Another great filtering question is a variation on the strategic question we suggest earlier, "If I did not do this activity/task already, would it help execute our plan if I started doing it today?" Answering these types of questions will identify those activities, tasks, reports, meetings, and projects that do not help you execute your plan. Then create a "stop doing" list for yourself and your team to help everyone stay focused on the most important activities. Your stop doing list often has a bigger impact on your team's ability to focus than your to do list.

Our clients' stop doing lists tend to cluster into three main areas: e-mail, reports, and meetings. Here is a list of the most common things they choose to stop:

- Stop continuing e-mail strings of more than three replies by picking up the phone or walking down the hall to talk to the other party.
- Stop audible e-mail alerts to prevent from constantly reacting to incoming e-mails.
- Stop using "Reply All" with e-mail.
- Stop allowing upward delegation by asking "What do you recommend?"
- Stop asking for reports that I do not use to make decisions and improvements.

STICK WITH IT

- Stop holding "meetings after the meetings"
- Stop holding and attending agendaless meetings
- Stop leaving most important items for last
- Stop doing recaps for late arrivals to meetings
- Stop scheduling meetings back-to-back each hour and instead schedule them for 45 minutes
- Stop requesting reports that I do not review or do not use to make decisions/changes.

One of our long-standing clients, National Motor Club, is a provider of roadside assistance and other safety and security benefits for its members. Soon after Matt Krzysiak was promoted to CEO, he showed leadership courage by rolling out an initiative called "the dumb things we do." It was a lighthearted, nonthreatening way to uncover goofy policies and inefficient processes that chipped away at customer loyalty, profit margins, and employee engagement. Over the course of a week, employees submitted short descriptions of any activities they felt did not add value and should be stopped or changed. All the feedback was compiled into a single list. Krzysiak shared the list with the entire company—with an open mind, no judgment, and lots of laughs—to reinforce his team's courage in revealing these issues. Then he involved the employees in fixing or stopping the "dumb things we do."

Like other winning leaders, Krzysiak understands that time, energy, and money are precious resources. If you spend them in one area, you don't have them available to spend in another. **Saying yes to something by default means saying no to something else.** Communicating this message enables your team to say no to the trivial many activities and stay focused on the vital few.

The 4 Ds

Of all the tools we've seen to help people stay focused and say no, the most effective one is, not surprisingly, the simplest. This tool is "old school," but don't let that fool you. It works and has been proven in the real world, so there is no gap between theory and practice. We call it the 4 Ds. It was originated by Dwight D. "Ike" Eisenhower, the World War II general who went on to become president of the United States. Ike used what is now called the Eisenhower method for setting priorities. He drew a square and divided it into four quadrants. One axis was a scale of important to unimportant; the other was urgent to not urgent.

	Important	**Unimportant**
Urgent	**DO** IT	**DELEGATE** IT
Not Urgent	**DEFER** IT	**DUMP** IT

After identifying the tasks confronting him, Ike categorized each one into the applicable quadrant. Tasks in the important/urgent quadrant were *done* immediately and by Ike personally. Tasks in the unimportant/urgent quadrant were *delegated*, and those in the important/not urgent quadrant were *deferred*, assigned due dates and done personally. Of course, anything falling in the unimportant/not urgent quadrant was *dumped* altogether.

When using the Eisenhower method, be sure to distinguish between urgent and important activities. Something that is important is something that is beneficial and should be accomplished—if not right away, then eventually. Something that is urgent is time-sensitive, but not necessarily important. Although important tasks are your top priorities, most of the time these are not the things that appear to be urgent. Don't be fooled into thinking that whatever seems urgent is worth taking your mind off your one thing for the day. Eisenhower's mantra was, "What's important is seldom urgent, and what's urgent is seldom important."

As we discuss in the previous chapter, the tyranny of the urgent is a fierce and powerful enemy of focus. Just because a task is urgent does not make it important. You and your team can "be like Ike" and know when to say no so that you can say yes to what is most important.

4 D Task Tracker
www.theLgroup.com/StickwithIt

Chapter At-a-Glance

- **Know when to say no**

  - Create decision hurdles in order to filter new opportunities.

  - Say no to activities, tasks, reports, meetings, and projects that do not directly support your plan.

  - Apply the 4 Ds: do it, delegate it, defer it, dump it.

I don't know the key to success, but the key to failure is trying to please everybody.

BILL COSBY, COMEDIAN, ACTOR, AUTHOR, EDUCATOR

9

Keep It Visible

In Chapter 7, we discuss the importance of having clarity about your one thing and of aligning your one thing with your team's, your department's, and ultimately your organization's top priority. This sounds like common sense, but it is not common practice as evidenced by these eye-opening findings from a Harris Interactive survey commissioned by FranklinCovey. The survey included 11,045 adult workers and found that:

- A majority of workers (51 percent) did not understand what they were supposed to do to help the organization achieve its goals.
- Only 19 percent of workers have clearly defined work goals.
- Only 9 percent believe that their work has a strong link to their organization's top priorities.[1]

These findings indicate a disconnect between an individual's activity and understanding and the organization's plan. It's easy to see how an explanation gap can lead to an execution gap. When we keep our plan visible and show team members how they contribute to it, a positive chain of events occurs:

Visible plan ⇒ transparency ⇒ trust and confidence ⇒ accountability and ownership ⇒ adherence to your plan ⇒ positive business impact

Our discussions with senior leaders revealed time and again the importance of keeping the organization's plan visible and ensuring that people understand the connection between that plan and their daily tasks. The Container Store is a great example. It sets the gold standard for internal communications and is perennially near the top of *Fortune* magazine's 100 best companies to work for. It can hardly "contain" itself when it comes to explaining the business and the plan to employees.

President Melissa Reiff says:

> *In order for us to fully execute with excellence, every single employee must be informed—or on the same page of the songbook as we like to say. We must consistently and transparently communicate with employees about simply everything. No secrets, no silos. This is our seventh foundational principle:* Communication IS leadership. *But it's a challenge. It's hard to breathlessly communicate the way we do. You must be totally committed. Equally important is that our leaders diligently follow up on the direction, the message and the details of the plan, always explaining the "whys" behind it.*[2]

We asked Reiff a half-dozen questions about how she and her team ensure adherence to their plans. Every one of her replies came back to communication—consistent, detailed, multichanneled communication with all employees. She feels so strongly about communicating all business information to the team that she is willing to risk some information falling into the wrong hands. Reiff considers it a small risk relative to the value of a highly informed and engaged workforce.[3]

Create a Communication Blueprint

To maintain visibility of your team's plan, you need to have an intentional communication scheme. Consider all available communication channels, such as memos/e-mails, videos, newsletters, home mailings, company intranet, staff meetings, town-hall chats, training sessions, focus groups, walk-arounds, company parties/celebrations, video boards, running banners on PCs, videoconferences, and any others that make sense for your organization's culture and operations. Select channels that are perceived as most reliable and credible by your team. Remember, the message is reinforced by the medium. For example, if you are announcing an important new product, communicating via e-mail might be perceived as matter of fact. It sends the message that the new product is not critical to the business. Alternatively, companywide or departmentwide meetings that include a presentation and an opportunity for employees to ask questions suggest that the time, effort, and preparation for these meetings are proportionate to the importance of a new product introduction.

Here are just a few ways our clients have maintained visibility for their organizations' purpose, vision, values, and strategies:

- Post video blogs from the CEO.
- Ask customers to give live testimonies about how the company's product or service positively affected their lives. (This is a real motivator!)
- Hang posters and banners throughout the workplace and in break areas.
- Give out or use as rewards: laptop stickers, hats, T-shirts, key chains, flash drives, coasters, mouse pads, or buttons.
- Leave an occasional all-company voice message.
- Share stories in newsletters, memos, and company blogs of outstanding performance or employees who are living company values. (Stories stick in readers' minds and really bring concepts to life.)
- Conduct "skip level" discussions in which executives meet with, talk with, and listen to team members several levels down in the organization.
- Use the vision, purpose, or strategy as a theme for annual meetings.

- Create reward or recognition programs for those who go above and beyond to help execute the strategy or live the values.
- Utilize the first three minutes of every meeting to discuss a particular value, the organization's purpose, or a specific strategy.

Frequency is also key when building a communication blueprint. Cindy Lewis is CEO of AirBorn, a client who manufactures high-reliability and custom electronics. She knows how to stick with her communication. Lewis uses the "six repetitions rule" when communicating important news, the idea being that you should not expect team members to fully understand or internalize any message until they hear it repeated at least six times. In Lewis's words, "After about six repetitions, we find the concept/message moves to long-term memory and then impacts behavior and habits."[4] This is not a statement about anyone's intelligence, but rather a statement about today's information-rich, time-poor, change-intensive workplace. Communicating a message at least six times also forces you to change it up to keep it interesting for your audience members (who all have different learning styles) while maintaining the integrity of your message.

Communication Plan Sample
www.theLgroup.com/StickwithIt

Maintain a Meeting Rhythm

Winning leaders leverage their meetings as platforms to continually communicate their plans. Mark Blinn is CEO of Flowserve, a client whose solutions help move, control, and protect the flow of materials in critical industries around the world. To effectively lead a global, multibillion-dollar business, Blinn maintains a robust meeting rhythm with the primary purpose of keeping top priorities visible. This creates downward and upward accountability from his department heads to the boardroom. His meeting rhythm includes:

- Weekly one-on-one updates with his team
- Biannual formal performance reviews (where there are no surprises because any issues have been addressed in the weekly updates)
- Detailed monthly operations reviews with his direct team and one level below
- Periodic strategy reviews
- Quarterly board of directors' meetings[5]

Here is a simple model for meeting rhythm that can be adapted to your team's needs, taking into account factors such as the maturity of your team, the location of team members, and the interdependence of the functions for which you are responsible. As you can see from the graphic below, the frequency, content, and duration of meetings are interrelated. To keep your team's tactical focus on their one thing, a brief but daily touch point is helpful. On the other end of the continuum, strategic issues require more time and involvement but typically occur only annually.

For example, using this model you might establish a meeting rhythm that looks like this:

- **Daily stand-up huddle** (5 to 10 minutes). Identify each team member's one thing for that day and combine it with any required coordination of efforts. Higher-level leaders might have this daily meeting with their executive assistant, key project managers, or department heads.

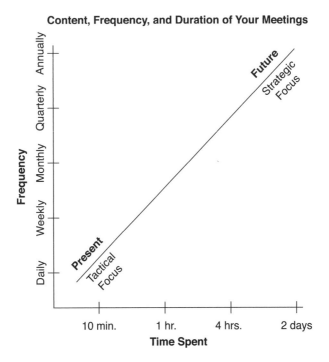

Content, Frequency, and Duration of Your Meetings

- **Weekly team update** (45 to 60 minutes). Discuss short-term initiatives and projects. Focus on those that are off track and identify actions to get them back on track, as well as the timing and resources needed to do so.

- **Monthly department dialogue** (60 to 90 minutes). Provide a brief look back at departmental performance over the previous month and reinforce the department's one thing for the coming month. Use this opportunity to recognize those who are living the values, demonstrating outstanding performance, and moving the department forward. Engage attendees with questions or solicit their input on a challenge or problem you need help solving. Use this time to get real work done, not to just share information.

- **Quarterly strategic review** (4 hours, offsite). Take a look at your key metrics (more on this in Chapter 13, "Balance Your

View"). Make adjustments to timing and resources for the most critical initiatives to ensure that they remain or get back on track.

- **Annual strategic planning** (2 days, offsite). The productivity of these meetings is directly related to the amount of preparation, so create a detailed agenda (with prework required of attendees) at least two weeks in advance. Topics should be future-focused, with a brief look back over the year to capture lessons learned. Topics might include adjusting your current strategy or developing a new one; assessing talent/succession planning; developing ways to improve execution capabilities; discussing game-changing initiatives like acquisitions, new products, consolidations, or divestitures.

Of course, your meeting rhythm should be mimicked by your direct reports with your teams (and so on down the organization) so that your message does not get bottlenecked below you. Your meeting rhythm typically becomes an important ritual for your team (more on rituals in Chapter 19, "Create Connections").

Winning leaders are able to find the right balance between maintaining a meeting rhythm and avoiding monotonous meetings. In any organization, it's easy for boredom to creep into recurring meetings, particularly those that follow a report-out format (i.e., each person gives an update). But it doesn't do any good to "check off" a weekly meeting if the team was "checked out" during the meeting. It takes a bit of leadership courage to occasionally try something new, mix things up, and go out on a limb to maintain engagement in meetings.

Elaine Agather has a keen understanding of this balance. As head of J.P. Morgan Private Bank's South Region, she maintains her own meeting rhythm with her team and also participates in a meeting rhythm with her peers across the globe. Agather is fully focused on customer service—connecting with and relating to customers. She knows that in order to transfer that focus to her team and colleagues, she must connect with them first. So it is part courage, part people-savvy, and part laserlike focus on customer service that drives her to mix things up in her meetings. She really upped the ante when she was asked to lead one of J.P. Morgan's global meetings of her peers and top executives via webcast. Agather decided to draw upon her first love, the rodeo! She wore her full rodeo regalia for the meeting.[6] To say that she broke the normal routine is putting it mildly. Do you think her fellow bankers were paying attention to her message? You bet they were.

Look for Yellow Cars

We have a special family tradition with our children. For their twelfth birthday, they each select any city in the continental United States to visit for a special celebration with just Mom and Dad—no siblings. A few years ago, we took our middle child to New York City to celebrate her twelfth birthday. Having been there many times ourselves, it is always fun to see the wonderment in a first-time visitor's eyes as she took in the lights of Times Square, the windows of the shops along Fifth Avenue, the view from the Empire State Building, and the ethnic richness of Chinatown and Little Italy.

Since our hotel was near Times Square, we walked a well-worn path down Broadway during our stay. Times Square really is the ultimate in sensory overload. After nearly a dozen trips down the same street, we noticed something new every time. Whatever item we were looking for seemed to magically appear even though we had previously walked past it numerous times without noticing—a souvenir shop, a deli, a street vendor selling scarves, a hot dog stand, live musicians, or Italian cannoli. Whatever we were looking for seemed to pop out from the array of visual stimuli of Times Square. This experience reminded us once again that **when you change the way you look at things, things change the way they look.**

The things we pay the most attention to reflect what we think about most. The reverse is also true. If we change what we think about, what we notice in our surroundings will change. For example, when was the last time you saw a yellow car that wasn't a taxi? Maybe last week or last month? Now that we have made you aware of yellow cars and you are thinking about them, you will start seeing more of them. Is there going to be a sudden invasion of bright yellow cars? Of course not. They've been there all along. The difference is that in the days ahead you will be thinking about them and, therefore, you will more readily notice yellow cars.

We call this connection between our thoughts and our attention "the yellow car phenomenon." This phenomenon is rooted in neuroscience. The reticular activating system (RAS) is the mechanism in the human brain that brings relevant information to your attention.[7] In essence, the RAS is the brain's filter between the subconscious and conscious mind. Without your being aware of it, the RAS sifts through the millions of pieces of information, stimuli, and data coming into your brain from all your senses. It then filters out the irrelevant and brings only the relevant information to your conscious mind.

So, the RAS decides what you focus your attention on. It allows your conscious mind to focus only on that which you've determined is useful right now. This explains why, on our walks down Broadway in New York City, we didn't notice the Italian cannoli when we were looking for scarves and vice versa, but once we were hungry we saw cannoli galore! And it's why you'll start seeing yellow cars now that we've planted the information in your RAS that yellow cars are relevant.

You can leverage the yellow car phenomenon to keep your plan visible at the strategic level and to keep your one thing visible at the tactical level. Here are some ways to make the RAS work for you:

When you focus on . . .	You will find . . .
The connection between the organization's plan and frontline tasks.	Chances to build bridges so that front-line employees better understand their contributions; new, innovative ways that frontline team members can execute the plan.
Your One Thing	Resources to help you complete it; opportunities to find others who excel at the same activity; ways to reinforce it with your team
Examples of sharp focus on your team	Best practices you can highlight for other team members to use; new tools that can sharpen focus; lessons from people outside of work who have sharp focus.

Keeping your plan visible improves your focus and, therefore, your adherence. Start by making your team's one thing its "yellow car." Is it selling opportunities, new applications for existing products, ways to cut costs, new markets to enter, building better products, finding a more efficient way to deliver? Whatever it is, talk about it, think about it, and keep it top-of-mind with your team. When you do, everyone will start seeing more opportunities and noticing more situations that relate to your yellow car. These things have always been there, but now you're paying attention to them. It's the power of focused attention. For proof, just count how many yellow cars you notice tomorrow.

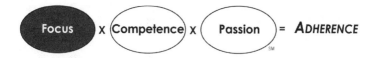

Chapter At-a-Glance

- **Keep it visible**
  - Create a communication blueprint using the six repetitions rule.
  - Maintain a meeting rhythm.
  - Look for "yellow cars."

_____

Genius is nothing but continued attention.

CLAUDE-ADRIEN HELVÉTIUS,
PHILOSOPHER

_____

10

Sharpening Personal Focus

D ave Thomas's (founder of Wendy's) life shows how a sharp focus can yield the results we desire. Given up for adoption soon after he was born, Dave's adoptive mother died when he was five. He spent the remainder of his childhood moving around as his adoptive father looked for employment. Never having had a traditional family, one of his earliest pleasures was eating at restaurants and watching families enjoying being together—a memory that focused all his efforts and ultimately fueled his success.

Dave worked at several restaurants as a teenager, even getting fired once when his employer discovered his young age. While he was in the tenth grade, he dropped out of school to work full time. Never losing sight of his goal to work in a restaurant, as soon as his army enlistment was up, Dave went to work at the Hobby House Restaurant.

Then, in 1962, Dave received an offer of a lifetime—if he could bring four Kentucky Fried Chicken restaurants out of the red, his boss would give him a whopping 45 percent of the business. Always focused and ready for a challenge, Dave went right to work—first reducing the menu to only a few choices and then using clever ads to bring business to the four restaurants. As business picked up and the restaurants became profitable, Dave opened four more locations.

Six short years after this challenge, 35-year-old Dave Thomas felt it was time to realize his life-long dream. In 1969, he opened his first Wendy's Old-Fashioned Hamburgers, naming his restaurant after his youngest daughter.

Dave worked tirelessly to grow the company, and today, Wendy's has grown to more than 6,500 restaurants worldwide. During the 1990s when Dave appeared in Wendy's commercials, a survey found that 90 percent of Americans knew who Dave Thomas was. With focus and perseverance, Dave far surpassed the dream of a little boy who, not having a real family of his own while a youngster, enjoyed seeing families dining together at his family restaurants.[1]

Focus Actions

Following are some actions that highly focused winners, like the late Dave Thomas, take to sharpen their focus. Put a check mark next to the actions you already execute with excellence.

— **Keep your goals visible at all times—literally.**

Keep your personal goals on your desk, posted to your laptop, in your wallet or purse, on your screen saver, on your bathroom mirror, on your refrigerator, and so on. This plants the seeds of success in your mind and focuses your attention on actions that will help you achieve your goals.

— **Make a list and check it twice**

Start each day with a list of what you need to achieve that day. Identify those vital few tasks that will have the biggest impact on your achieving your top goal for the day and do those tasks first. This way, if the rest of the day gets lost to the trivial many, your day will still be a victory.

— **Eat that frog**

As success expert and best-selling author Brian Tracy says, "If the first thing you do when you wake up in the morning is eat a live frog, then nothing worse can happen for the rest of the day!"[2] Brian's idea is that if you start your day doing your most unpleasant but necessary task, the rest of your day will be a walk in the park. Discipline is doing what you have to do so you can do what you want to do. Life rewards action, so dive in and get to work. Future tasks appear larger and more overwhelming than they really are.

— Take baby steps

Divide your big goals into small steps to help you focus on the next action you need to take to achieve your ultimate goal. This builds momentum and confidence while leaving little room for nonvalue-added activity. Taking baby steps also keeps you from being "paralyzed" by what appears to be an overwhelming goal.

— Control your inputs

Whatever your mind hears from others, and especially from you, it records and stores. The mind doesn't discriminate between what is good and what is harmful—it collects and remembers all input. Control your inputs by monitoring what you watch on television, starting your day with an inspiring story, and spending time with people who share your focus. Most importantly, control what you say to yourself to ensure that you are planting positive expectations in your mind.

Close the Gap

Start closing the knowing-doing gap by reviewing the actions above and the at-a-glance summary. Then, write down:

One action you can take today to sharpen your *team* focus:

_____

_____

One action you can take today to sharpen your *personal* focus:

_____

_____

FOCUS At-a-Glance

- **Keep it simple**
  - Think in threes to simplify strategies, metrics, messages, and actions.
  - Apply the 80/20 principle to focus on the 20 percent that are your vital few.
- **Identify your one thing**
  - Decide what is most important—the one activity that most directly help you execute your plan.
  - Align your one thing with the organization's most important priority.
  - Ask your team, "What is the most valuable thing you can do right now?"
- **Know when to say no**
  - Create decision hurdles to filter new opportunities.
  - Say no to activities, tasks, reports, meetings, and projects that do not directly support your plan.
  - Apply the Four Ds: do it, delegate it, defer it, dump it.
- **Keep it visible**
  - Create a communication blueprint using the six repetitions rule.
  - Maintain a meeting rhythm.
  - Look for "yellow cars."

PART III

Competence

$$\text{Focus} \times \text{Competence} \times \text{Passion} = \textit{ADHERENCE}$$

W e love to watch the Olympics. Nothing stirs the emotions like seeing a lifelong journey of sacrifice and overcoming adversity culminating in either the joy of victory or the agony of defeat. Like nearly a billion others worldwide, we are personally drawn to the athletes' stories. Not only are these athletes testaments to the human spirit, but they are also living examples of competence as we define it in the adherence equation. Only when we see one of those back-story minidocumentaries highlighting a particular Olympian do we more fully appreciate all it takes to build world-class competence. We learn about gut-wrenching daily training regimens, strict nutritional standards, rigorous mental discipline, top-notch training equipment, reams of collected data, various supporting relationships, and even past adversities that motivate the Olympian. It is an intentionally developed set of systems and processes designed to produce a golden victory.

Whether in the Olympics or in business, outsiders tend to see only the outcome of competence—a winning sprinter crossing the finish line or a winning salesperson closing a big deal. What we do not see is everything it took to build that level of performance. As you may recall, we use "competence" in the broadest sense of the word. The competence component of the adherence equation describes more than just skills and knowledge. It encompasses work processes, systems, roles, measures, feedback, training, expectations, and mental preparation—everything a team uses to stick with its plan and measure its progress.

Competence is about equipping your team so they can be productive. Hay Group research shows that nine out of ten employees are committed to success, but it also indicates that fewer than two-thirds of them believe they are as productive as they could be. The very best organizations, the world's most admired companies, build competence and productivity by:

- Working "smarter," that is, simplifying work processes
- Creating systems and processes that encourage employees to become part of the solution
- Prioritizing work/life balance issues to sustain performance and avoid burnout
- Ensuring that employees' skills remain aligned with changing work demands[1]

Competence answers the "how" question—how will you adhere to your strategy? Our most successful clients get the answer by addressing these four adherence accelerators needed for building competence:

1. Treasure your talent by selecting the right people to begin with and then developing and coaching your talent for success.
2. Define work systems and processes to efficiently and predictably get results.
3. Balance your view between the details and the big picture, and between leading and lagging business indicators.
4. Boost accountability with specific language, expectations, and consequences.

We look at each of these adherence accelerators in the next four chapters.

A competent leader can get efficient service from poor troops, while on the contrary an incapable leader can demoralize the best of troops.

JOHN J. PERSHING,
FORMER BRIGADIER GENERAL

11

Treasure Your Talent

t's hard to lose when you have great talent, and it's hard to win without it. In fact, in a study of *Fortune's* world's most admired companies, one of the three common themes among top performers in every industry was "achieving success through people." The study's authors concluded, "'Our people are our greatest asset' may sound like a platitude, but our research shows that for the World's Most Admired Companies, it's core to their success."[2]

In today's fast-moving business environment, competitors can quickly neutralize nearly every advantage you have, whether it's your distribution channels, technology, access to capital, or lower production costs. Every advantage, that is, except your talent. While you should value all of your talent, it's crucial that you value your top talent. **Top talent is your greatest asset; whereas weak talent is your greatest liability.** High-performing organizations put dedicated resources behind proactive efforts to identify stellar talent, both internally and externally. Internally, talent rises to the top through training programs, key projects, outstanding effort, sound thinking, and solid decision making. When you make "finding great internal talent" your yellow car, you will discover more than you ever thought was available. After all, at the end of the day, your success is based more on what your people do than on what you do.

Mining for top talent externally requires specific, focused effort. For example, talent-driven organizations perform one or more of these talent-mining activities:

- Maintain a list of talented candidates they would like to hire;
- Take top external candidates to lunch even if they don't have current job openings for them;
- Use internship programs to "test drive" new talent;
- Use a dedicated "superstar" recruiter (internal employee or external firm) who looks exclusively for key players who can help the organization move forward.

Mining for talent using these approaches enables you to build a database of top talent, which then allows you to quickly respond to a special organizational need or to proactively hire a superstar for a new initiative that will take you to the next level. Often, however, there isn't someone in your "superstar database" who meets a current need on your team. In those cases, you have to select smart.

Select Smart

Selecting top talent is a prerequisite to building competence and adhering to your plan. Team member selection is the ultimate pay-now or pay-later leadership proposition. Select smart now, and you will reap the benefits of a winning team later. Select fast and haphazardly now, and you will pay the price later of increased turnover, underperforming teams, a diluted culture, and a drain on managerial time.

Research indicates that the direct cost of turnover can be as high as 50 to 60 percent of an employee's annual salary, with the fully loaded cost of turnover between 90 and 200 percent of annual salary.[3] To illustrate the importance of selecting smart, let's be ultraconservative and assume just a 50 percent total turnover cost and employees with a $40,000 annual salary. The math is simple and compelling: Reduce turnover by just 10 employees, and you add $200,000 back to your bottom line! Although there are many things you can do as a leader to reduce turnover, making the right selection decision will give you the biggest bang for your buck.

Top 10 Employee Selection Mistakes and Solutions
www.theLgroup.com/StickwithIt

We have found a nearly zero correlation between years of experience hiring people and effective selection, meaning that experienced leaders are no more effective than rookie leaders at selecting winning talent. In fact, experienced leaders are more likely to rely solely on gut feel and stray from proven selection practices. Experience and intuition are important, but so are reliable and valid ways to collect data, such as testing, simulations, behavioral interviews, and work samples. No single aspect of the selection process should be relied on exclusively; rather, multiple methods should be used and weighted based on the job requirements and your organization's values.

Smart selection is all about finding people who are a good fit for your team. The most expensive clothing you can buy from the most exclusive store won't look good if it doesn't fit you. The same is true with your talent. It has to fit your team and your organization. The best talent will represent both a skills fit with the job and a culture fit with your team. We rarely see a misfit of skills. In most cases, it's a straightforward process to determine whether a candidate has the required technical job skills like project management, data analysis, sales, planning, and so on. The bigger challenge is in assessing the "softer" skills that affect team culture, such as leadership, decision making, collaboration, communication, and customer service. These softer skills must support your team culture rather than undermine it, so reliably assessing soft skills is vital to your ability to ultimately adhere to your plan.

A culture misfit can cause more damage to your team than a skills misfit. Therefore, we advise clients to reverse the common process of screening for skills first and then confirming culture fit later. This reversal enables clients to ensure a culture fit before they assess skills. Of course, an initial look at a résumé generally screens out candidates who are not even in the "skills ballpark." Southwest Airlines exemplifies this reversal with its "hire for attitude and train for skills" approach. It hires for culture fit first and foremost and then trains for necessary skills. (Southwest is quick to point out that its pilots are the exception to this process!) It is no coincidence that Southwest consistently has one of the lowest employee turnover rates and the highest levels of employee satisfaction in their industry.[4]

One of the best ways to ensure smart selection is with a process we call 3 x 3 x 3. It is based on the idea that the more data points you capture, the smarter the selection decision. Since interviewing is like a first date—everyone is on their best behavior—3 x 3 x 3 necessitates that candidates be seen multiple times in multiple situations by multiple people. This process ensures that the organization considers three final candidates for each job opening and that the three candidates are each interviewed three times by three different interviewers. In the example below, three candidates are seen by three interviewers (Ryan, Cheryl, and Matt) as shown:

	1st Interview	2nd Interview	3rd Interview
Candidate #1	Ryan	Matt	Cheryl
Candidate #2	Cheryl	Ryan	Matt
Candidate #3	Matt	Cheryl	Ryan

The 3 x 3 x 3 process provides three perspectives on three candidates over three interviews. Candidates get more comfortable as the process progresses, and as a result, they express more unfiltered thoughts and behaviors (i.e., their true colors). This process more closely simulates the evolution of a relationship and provides more valid data points upon which to base a hiring decision. The 3 x 3 x 3 method also lets candidate know that you are serious about whom you hire and can cause them to decide to remove themselves from the interview process.

Development—a Perpetual Priority

To treasure your talent, selecting smart is necessary but not sufficient. The training, coaching, and exposure you provide to team members is a strong predictor of your future business results (more on leading indicators in Chapter 13, "Balance Your View").

Organizations that take a long-term view realize that developing talent is a perpetual priority rather than a list of training topics to be checked off. Below is a sample training model of how a winning organization might treasure its talent with topics that build skills at various levels of leadership: leading self, leading individuals, leading teams and leading organizations. The result is measurable competence at each skill level before an employee is elevated to the next level of development.

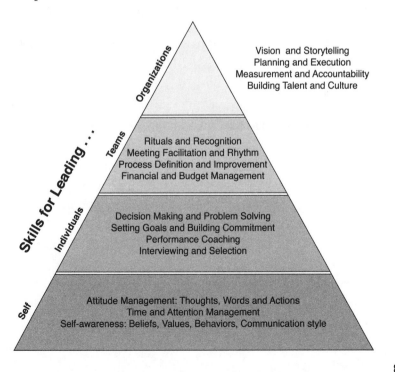

Organizations
Vision and Storytelling
Planning and Execution
Measurement and Accountability
Building Talent and Culture

Teams
Rituals and Recognition
Meeting Facilitation and Rhythm
Process Definition and Improvement
Financial and Budget Management

Individuals
Decision Making and Problem Solving
Setting Goals and Building Commitment
Performance Coaching
Interviewing and Selection

Self
Attitude Management: Thoughts, Words and Actions
Time and Attention Management
Self-awareness: Beliefs, Values, Behaviors, Communication style

Skills for Leading . . .

For example, The Hartford is a 200+-year-old insurance company. You don't survive (and thrive) that long without knowing how to change and adhere to a plan. The common thread across two centuries is that The Hartford knows how to equip its people for success. For example, the company's enterprise operations organization developed, and continues to enhance, a leadership tool kit to accomplish this. The tool kit is as robust as any operations manual, but it's specifically for leaders. It addresses coaching, roles, decision making, change management—in short, it defines The Hartford way of leading. And it's all online to provide equal access for those who choose to elevate their leadership. It has a great high-tech, high-touch balance with master coaches assigned to each division to support effective use of all the leadership tools that are available online. Leaders are fully equipped for success.[5]

Just as smart selection is only part of the solution for building competence, training is only part of the solution for developing your talent. The Hartford and other winning organizations realize that coaching is another important part of the process. All sports teams have a coach. The coach defines the players' roles, trains them to excel, provides feedback on performance, and offers tips and tools to boost performance. The coach does all this with one goal in mind—winning. In business, being a coach is core to the leader's role and certainly crucial to the team's ability to win. In fact, **winning leaders coach good employees to become better people**—they equip them for success at work and at home.

Sometimes we get so drawn to new approaches and technologies that we forget to do the basics (again, the knowing-doing gap). Employee coaching is one such example. Despite new techniques, assessments, and technologies that have been developed to help us coach more effectively, the fact remains that we are dealing with human beings. And as humans at work, we share fundamental needs that have never changed, regardless of our generation, geography, nationality, or gender. We all want to be informed, we want our opinions to matter, we want to be involved in creating changes and improvements, and finally we want to be acknowledged for our efforts. When they're coaching employees, winning leaders cut through the clutter and address these needs in four simple steps: explain, ask, involve, and appreciate.

1. **Explain:** Clearly describe why you need something done or why something needs to change. Answering the "why" questions is a key motivator—it gives meaning to our work.

2. **Ask:** Confirm understanding on the employee's part and do not proceed until the coach and the employee are perfectly clear. Listen 80 percent and talk 20 percent.

3. **Involve:** Discuss ideas for potential solutions and approaches.

4. **Appreciate:** Recognize positive movement or effort in order to encourage continued progress toward the agreed-upon goal.

As you progress through each step of this coaching process, you elevate your employee's performance. Let's see how a team leader, Jill, coaches an employee, Shane, using these four steps:

> *Jill:* Hey, Shane. I'm glad I bumped into you. I wanted to talk to you about something. We really need to improve our response time on special orders. *(Jill is explaining.)*
>
> *Shane:* Okay, I understand. *(Shane is simply observing.)*
>
> *Jill:* You're on the front lines with this issue. Why do you think our response time has increased lately? *(Jill is asking for input.)*
>
> *Shane:* Well, the new system migration has had its bumps. But I think the bigger issue is that we weren't prepared for the recent promotional campaign to our VIP customers. Our call volume from VIPs has increased by 40 percent for special orders over the same period last quarter. *(Shane is now participating.)*
>
> *Jill:* We need to discuss your ideas on how we can get back on track. Our response time has a direct impact on our bottom line, so I'll give you whatever support you need

to take care of this. *(Jill is explaining the impact on the business and involving Shane in finding a solution.)*

Shane: That sounds great. Let me send you some initial recommendations before our meeting. I'm confident we can identify a good solution and implement it quickly. *(Now, Shane is committed to solving the problem.)*

Jill: *(After the solution is implemented).* That was a great job, Shane. I really appreciate the way you took the initiative to explore solutions and make them happen. *(Jill is demonstrating her appreciation for Shane and for his performance.)*

Shane: Thanks, Jill! It was great to feel like I made a real difference. I've already proposed a process to the marketing department that will keep us in the loop and prevent this problem in the future. *(Shane is taking ownership of the problem.)*

When we build competence, we build confidence. Confidence is a vital asset for any winning team, and we go a long way to building it when we treasure our talent.

---

4 Steps for Winning Coaches
www.theLgroup.com/StickwithIt

Chapter At-a-Glance

- **Treasure talent**
  - Select smart—use the 3 x 3 x 3 process.
  - Treat employee development as a perpetual priority.
  - Coach for success with four steps: explain, ask, involve, and appreciate.

It's possible to fly without motors,
but not without knowledge and skill.

Wilbur Wright, Inventor
and Aviation Pioneer

12

Get Systematic

Military operations epitomize clear, paint-by-numbers systems, processes, and roles. Lee observed this firsthand when he spent a weekend aboard the USS *Abraham Lincoln* about 100 miles offshore as it prepared for deployment. This aircraft carrier, the proud flagship of the navy's fleet, is a floating city. More than 5,000 sailors work and live on it. They perform the most complex flight operations under the most tumultuous conditions, day and night, with zero degree of freedom. The cost of an error is tens of millions of dollars in damaged navy assets or even loss of life. No *Top Gun* movie scene here. This is the real danger zone with no room for error.

This type of environment demands a systematic way of getting results and nothing less than full adherence to a plan. In addition, carrier operations are performed mostly by 20-year-old enlisted sailors. That's the power of getting systematic. It elevates the average. In other words, work systems increase the average performance of team members and boost the predictability of results, thereby building team competence.

Work systems include any defined, methodical, repeatable way of doing work and making decisions. They should create positive habits for your team. Systems help you predictably and efficiently perform ongoing activities and tasks such as, making important decisions, prioritizing work, developing new products and services, developing prospects, delivering on time, planning new projects, selecting and developing employees, measuring performance, serving customers, and communicating with each other. Creating replicable work systems equips your team for consistent execution. Even the best talents can look like they are in a circus fire-drill skit if clear roles and work systems are lacking.

Long-time client, Andrew Levi, is CEO of Aztec Systems, a technology services firm. Levi is a visionary leader who has spent 20 years incubating, building, running, buying, and selling technology businesses. He knows that a systematic way of doing things creates a competitive advantage and value in the marketplace. In his words, "Without a 'paint-by-numbers' approach to work, people will invent their own Mona Lisa . . . and most businesses do not need a Mona Lisa. People want to do the right thing. The problem occurs when the organization has not defined what 'the right thing' is and how to perform it."[1]

Work systems can develop by default or by accident, but the most valuable work systems are intentionally designed to support and drive your operation. Ask yourself, "What work systems can I implement to help my team members consistently execute their routine tasks?" Here are some examples of effective work systems (some of which we discuss in prior chapters):

- Daily huddle to confirm that everyone is clear about their one thing.
- Regular performance reviews to ensure that each team member is adhering to the plan.
- 3 x 3 x 3 candidate interviewing process to make smart selection decisions.
- Discussion of what you should stop, start, and keep doing after each project to identify lessons learned.
- Exception reports that identify only tasks that are off-plan (versus reports that include data about every initiative).
- Periodic visits with customers by noncustomer-facing team members to ensure focus on whom they ultimately serve and their needs.

- Evaluation of project checkpoints/milestones to reveal warning signs of potential problems.

Implementing these types of work systems builds competence throughout the organization and helps you stick with your plan.

Collaborate with Clear Roles

In today's increasingly complex business world, most organizational structures incorporate a matrix element. Gone are the days of traditional functional or divisional structures, particularly for businesses with multiple products, services and/or locations. "Managing the matrix" is a way of life. Organization charts have more dotted lines than a Los Angeles freeway. As a result, collaboration is critical for building competence in today's organizations. The word says it all—"colabor"—to work together.

Winning organizations understand the importance of clarifying what *collaboration* means and looks like for all team members. First, collaboration should not be confused (but often is) with consensus. **Collaboration is a way of working together, whereas consensus is a form of decision making.** Allowing collaboration to morph into consensus can slow decision making. Sliding down the slippery slope of consensus will put the brakes on your business and halt progress on your plan. And in a speed-craved marketplace, that's the kiss of death.

Also, to collaborate well, team members must have clearly defined roles. There are plenty of models and acronyms that address who is responsible, consulted with, informed, makes decisions, and performs tasks. Again, simplicity is key. We suggest simple language and definitions that help your team focus on getting results. Here is one set of collaboration roles we recently defined for a highly matrixed organization:

- **Lead the team:** The person *ultimately responsible* for the completion of a project, and the one who assigns tasks and resources. There can be only one lead per project/initiative, and she or he makes final decisions.

- **Do the work:** Those who *directly perform the tasks*. Doers collaborate with subject matter experts as necessary.

- **Share expertise:** The person who *provides subject matter expertise* as requested by the lead or doers. This typically involves two-way communication about best practices, customer needs, and alternative approaches.

- **Get informed:** Those who are *kept up-to-date* on progress by doers and leaders, often only on completion of milestones. This typically involves one-way communication.

For true collaboration to work, we must let roles, not egos, drive our actions. On any given project, a team member can play different roles. So you might be getting informed on today's project and lead a team for next month's project. Excellent collaboration requires courage, trust and humility: courage to lead and do after hearing input from others; humility to share our expertise and then follow the decision someone else makes; and trust in our teammates to be informed of their progress.

Define clear collaboration roles within your team and watch your competence and adherence grow.

Innovate Daily

To execute consistently, we must improve consistently. Execution is not static; rather, it is a dynamic process. We must learn as we go. It's the only way to survive and thrive over the long haul. Although it may appear counterintuitive, the way we innovate can be systematized, or imbedded into our team culture.

Our teams are full of untapped ideas and creativity, much more than we ever capture. If we take a programmatic approach, most employees' ideas will get stuck in the proverbial suggestion box. The traditional suggestion box promotes complaining, anonymity, and abdication of responsibility—clearly not the hallmarks of innovation and competence. Employees from companies such as Bayer Pharmaceuticals, GM,

Starbucks, Dana Corp., Milliken & Company, Toshiba, Technicolor, and Boardroom, Inc., have generated thousands of ideas per year. This is *not* achieved by using a suggestion box. These organizations achieve innovation by tapping into team members' unlimited pool of ideas and creativity. This is not about ideas for ideas' sake. It is about soliciting ideas to improve productivity, reduce costs, increase speed, create new products, and eliminate waste.

In their book *The Phoenix Effect*, corporate turnaround specialists Carter Pate and Harlan Platt point out that the payoff for routine process improvements can be huge. These changes are typically inexpensive, can be implemented quickly, and involve transitions from less efficient to more efficient methods. They conclude: "One of the least expensive yet most frequently overlooked weapons in the corporate renewal armory is altering the functional processes of a business."[2]

Winning organizations systematize and streamline processes by applying the following innovation principles:

- Ideas are part of everyone's job.
- The process for submitting ideas is quick and easy.
- Ideas are reviewed by people who know the job and who will be directly affected if the ideas are implemented.
- Ideas are evaluated thoroughly, and decisions are made quickly.
- Feedback to the employee who suggested the idea is quick and complete. In most cases, he or she should be involved in the decision, so feedback is instantaneous.
- Whenever possible, and in most cases, ideas are implemented immediately.
- The process for managing ideas, as informal as it may be, is always monitored and improved.

The key to daily innovation is to think small. Small ideas enable you to focus on the details of your business. Consistent execution is a result of getting the details right through constant tweaking of work systems. In many cases, it is literally impossible to improve performance (e.g., speed, service, quality, costs) beyond a certain level without small ideas. Small ideas are actually better than big ideas because small ideas:

- Are much more likely to stay proprietary and create sustainable competitive advantage since they are situation-specific. (Besides, your competitors are most likely looking for the next big idea. Let them wait for their grand slam while you hit a thousand singles.)
- Help create a culture that values ideas and the people who have them, resulting in ownership behavior.
- Keep your team engaged on a daily basis.
- Facilitate rapid and continuous organizational learning and improvements based on that learning.
- Are the best sources of big ideas—the Post-It Note came from a small idea to find better glue.

Small ideas make a big difference because they improve processes that are repeated over and over again. Here are some examples of small ideas that made a big difference for our clients: "If I highlight off-budget line items on my report, the executive committee can more quickly and efficiently focus on those areas of concern." "While I'm waiting for our drivers to check in their shipments at our store's receiving dock, I sweep out their trucks so they can make quicker turn-arounds at our distribution center." "If we eliminate the cover page on internal faxes, we will save 150 pieces of paper per month." No single small idea will transform your team, but all of them together will create a culture of innovation and competence. The following idea tracker example reflects the elegant simplicity with which we can innovate daily:

My Team's Idea Tracker

Originator	Idea	Priority	Implementer	Complete by/Status
Donna	Put yellow tape on the first step into the mailroom to prevent people from tripping on the step.	High	Donna	By noon this Friday.
Jay	Pack a preset portable box with meeting supplies that can be easily taken to off-site meetings to avoid paying hotel fees for these items. We spent $1,500 to rent these items last year.	High	Jay	One business week prior to the next off-site meeting.
Rose	Post our chart of account codes on our intranet so managers can correctly code invoices and reduce the number of late payments to key vendors. Currently 50% of our invoices must be returned or corrected, each taking and average of 3 additional days to process.	Medium	Rose with help Peter in IT department	By 5 p.m. ET on the 31st of this month.

Idea Tracker Template
www.theLgroup.com/StickwithIt

You can increase the usefulness of the ideas you receive by asking your team for the kinds of ideas you need. For instance, you may have a particular area that needs improvement for that week, month, or quarter (your one thing). Then set an idea goal for your employees—

perhaps one small idea per month. Use early wins to reinforce the benefits of daily innovation, build momentum, and spread enthusiasm.

Avoid approaching this like another program, or you might end up trapped inside the suggestion box. Instead, work to create a culture of innovation. Take it slow—this may be a fundamental shift for your team. And remember, you are dealing with small ideas, so take small steps. Daily innovation is a big idea that will put you a big step ahead of your competition.

Chapter At-a-Glance

- **Get systematic**
  - Create repeatable work systems.
  - Collaborate with clear roles.
  - Innovate daily—what's the small idea?

For the first 25 years of my life I wanted freedom.
For the next 25 years I wanted order.
For the last 25 years I realized that order is freedom.

WINSTON CHURCHILL,
FORMER PRIME MINISTER
OF GREAT BRITAIN

13

Balance Your View

L ast summer we took our family on a vacation to Italy to celebrate two family milestones that occurred simultaneously—our twenty-fifth wedding anniversary and our oldest child's graduation from high school. This trip with our children was particularly fun since Lee's father grew up in Italy (Colan is short for Colantuono). One of the highlights was seeing the glassblowing artists on Murano Island near Venice. We watched in amazement as they transformed globs of molten glass into beautifully detailed sculptures that would later become pieces of an awe-inspiring chandelier—all in just 30 seconds!

It was incredible how these artists balanced their view. They clearly had a vision of the final product, the chandelier, as well as a vision of each individual sculpture. With these in mind, they executed a multitude of maneuvers—some minute and others sweeping—to bring their vision to fruition.

Like Murano glassblowers, winning leaders expertly balance their view. Our most successful clients balance their view two different ways. First, they understand the value of seeing both the big picture and the details of their operation. Second, they realize that they must pay attention to both leading and lagging indicators of performance. Let's examine each of these in more depth.

Big Picture and Details

A common misperception among leaders is that once you get to a certain level, you should consider only a 30,000-foot perspective (i.e., big picture) of your business. Although a high-level perspective is necessary for leadership success, it must be accompanied by an in-depth understanding of your team's operation (e.g., your drivers of cost, profit, quality, and customer satisfaction). **When we make a habit of ignoring the little things, we eventually end up ignoring the big things.** Don't misinterpret this as micromanagement. We are discussing leadership knowledge, not leadership activity.

Your car provides a helpful analogy for understanding the importance of both big picture and detailed information. Just as your car's dashboard tells you speed, fuel level, and engine temperature, your organizational dashboard tells you if sales are up 5 percent, productivity is down, or project deliverables are on schedule. While dashboard knowledge is important for understanding broad metrics and the general direction of your operation, it is less helpful for identifying specific actions, improvements, and adjustments that will help your team run more smoothly. For that kind of information, you have to look "under the hood." Looking under your car's hood provides insight into why your car is running hot, why it veers to the right, and why it's not starting as quickly as it should. Under-the-hood knowledge about your team gives you specific information with respect to a given job, time, place, and set of circumstances. Winning leaders consider both dashboard and under-the-hood knowledge. They understand that by the time a warning light on your dashboard starts blinking, you already have a problem under the hood.

You can get under-the-hood knowledge either by checking under the hood yourself or from people who are currently working under the hood (those on the front lines). Former Apple CEO Steve Jobs understood the importance of "getting his hands dirty" and checking under the hood of his business. He reportedly was personally involved in customer service on a regular basis, communicating with customers by phone and by e-mail about their problems, hardware issues, and pricing questions.[1] His balanced view helped create innovative products that have literally transformed the way we live and work.

One of our clients, Bob Bunker, CEO of Medical Staffing Network, also artfully balances his view of the big picture and the details. Bunker likes to harken back to his military days when he's looking under the hood. He refers to his field offices as the FEBA (forward edge of battle area). It's a vivid reminder to his corporate team that the field offices are where the business battle is won on a daily basis. Bunker has been known to spend much of his time on the FEBA listening to his field team and customers and supporting them both. He says, "Getting on the FEBA allows me to see and feel the daily processes and ponder process reengineering opportunities, technology applications and better appreciate the interdependencies of our corporate and customer systems as a whole."[2] This under-the-hood knowledge ultimately helps Bunker take a more complete view of the business.

Bunker gains under-the-hood knowledge by asking his team questions like:

- What are your time killers?
- What situations or processes make it difficult to get your jobs done?
- What things would you change if you were in my position?
- What can I do better/more of to support your success?

By simply asking questions, your employees will reveal challenges and opportunities that could potentially take you months or years to identify. A word of caution: Don't ask if you're not going to listen. Asking without listening builds cynicism and drains your efforts to build competence and to adhere to your plans. Asking questions and then really listening demonstrates personal respect, obtains buy-in, and makes people feel valued in a way that financial rewards cannot. **Winning leaders listen at least 50 percent of the time.** Andrew Levi, the client we mention in the last chapter, has done a tremendous amount of leading, presenting, pitching, directing, persuading, and explaining in his efforts to build winning cultures and businesses.

When asked about the topic of listening, he directly replied, "He who talks the most loses."[3]

Leading and Lagging Indicators

Winning leaders also balance their view by looking at both leading and lagging indicators of performance. Every team has a variety of performance indicators. Teams that adhere to their plans understand the different types of indicators, what they mean, and how to balance them. Consider a measurement continuum. The two ends represent the two types of performance indicators. *Lagging indicators* are the results of your team's *past* performance—they enable you to see if your activities produced the desired outcomes. *Leading indicators* are the drivers of your team's *future* performance—they help you predict future success and problems.

The graphic below illustrates leading and lagging measures at the organization level. However, as you delve into each of these areas of measurement (financial, customer, process and people), we also find leading and lagging indicators within them. For example, within people measures, level of engagement today is a leading indicator that predicts turnover rate in the future. Also, within the financial measures, the collections today help predict your free cash flow tomorrow. Likewise, the effectiveness of your customer problem resolution today helps predict customer loyalty in the future.

Financial Measures	Customer* Measures	Process Measures	People Measures
• Revenues • Costs • Profits	• Complaint Resolution • Customer Satisfaction • Customer Retention	• Quality • Cycle Time • Productivity • Response Time	• Employee Satisfaction • Employee Development • Employee Retention

Lagging Indicators ←——————————————→ *Leading Indicators*

Past   **Future**

Internal and external

Balanced Scoreboard Sample
www.theLgroup.com/StickwithIt

John Walker is COO and CFO for KidKraft, a leading creator, manufacturer, and distributor of children's furniture and toys worldwide. KidKraft has been an industry pioneer for 40 years. Walker is particularly skilled at balancing the types of knowledge he seeks. Walker summed it up like this: "If you want to know what's going on in your business, talk to your customer service reps and your collections reps."[4] Walker understands these two functions offer direct customer information from opposite ends (leading and lagging) of the customer life cycle.

Economic and competitive pressures force many leaders to focus on lagging indicators, typically financial ones. Of course, it's important to consider lagging indicators to know how well you have performed in the past. However, you must balance your view with leading indicators that indicate how your organization will perform 6, 9, or 12 months from now. A singular focus on lagging indicators gives you little opportunity for corrective action if your team drifts off course. Effective leaders look at both lagging and leading indicators of performance. This balanced view enables them to know what *did* happen and also anticipate what *will* happen.

For example, a company that sold software designed to manage computer assets was growing so fast that it became enamored of its revenue growth (a lagging indicator) to the exclusion of leading indicators such as employee development and service quality. Since its investors were happy, this focus solely on lagging indicators went on for nearly two years. As a result, the company thought that the light it saw at the end of the tunnel was its bright future. Instead, it was an oncoming train. The company's meteoric rise was matched only by its swift decline. Because employees were not being trained and developed, they were either ill-equipped to take on new responsibilities or disillusioned. Some left the company, and those who remained were not able to maintain expected quality levels. This took little time to translate into lower customer satisfaction which, in a very competitive market, quickly resulted in much lower customer retention. And we all know what happens to revenues when we lose customers. Unfortunately in this case, even a diligent rebalancing of the company's view and the resulting corrective action was too little too late.

As the captain of your team's ship, keep a balanced view of your team's performance to increase your competency and adhere to your plan. Chart your course (high-level perspective) and ensure that the deck is clean (details). While on your journey, check the wake of your ship (lagging indicators) and keep an eye on the horizon ahead (leading indicators).

Keep Score

Have you ever noticed the intensity difference when you play a game for fun compared to "playing for keeps"? Our family frequently plays Ping-Pong in our game room. It's a fun and easy game for all ages. It's easy and pretty relaxed to just volley back and forth, but there are visible changes once we start keeping score—greater intensity, better focus, more energy, and more winning shots. You can observe the same in any sport and certainly in your organization.

In Chapter 4, we outline the six simple questions that create a winning plan. Question 5 was, "How will we measure our success?" You have to keep score in order to know whether you are winning. You can keep score on your revenue, profitability, customer satisfaction, quality, prospect pipeline, cost per sales, employee engagement, defects, inventory, call-center response time, and so on. There certainly is no lack of things to measure. To keep it simple, **measure only what matters most.** Do not measure everything. You can use the 80/20 principle here. Which 20 percent of the measures tell you 80 percent of the story? Those are the measures you want to track.

Of course, if you are going to keep score, you need a scoreboard. You will want to design a scoreboard that is simple and clear, resonates with your team, and is easy to update. It's also a chance to be creative and visual with your team. Your scoreboard doesn't have to be a lackluster summary of your monthly business report showing key measures. Use your scoreboard to tell a clear and compelling story in as few words and numbers as possible. Consider some of these scoreboard formats:

- Visual thermometer with a rising mercury line to show progress
- Traffic light (red, yellow, and green indicators to show if you are off-plan, slightly off-plan, or on-plan, respectively)
- A jar of jellybeans to illustrate percentage of completion
- Emoticons (☺, ☹) or visual indicators such as thumbs up/thumbs down next to each goal. (These work great for movie reviews and Facebook, so why not use them to help your team quickly see the score?)
- A picture of an actual scoreboard to keep track of revenues, new deals, market share, customer referral, or whichever metrics are most important to your team.

Scoreboard Review Process
www.theLgroup.com/StickwithIt

Keeping your scoreboard updated is critical. If your scoreboard doesn't contain the current score or is not seen as a reliable reflection of reality, it will no longer serve as a motivator, and it will lose its power to influence behavior. Your scoreboard must be current to be compelling.

Sears has taken the concept of scoreboarding to a whole new level. By taking cues from gaming hits like Angry Birds and Fantasy Football, Sears created a platform to "game-ify" the performance of key roles in its stores. Using basic gaming principles, it created a real-time, nationwide leader board to see who is the best from Seattle to Florida. Furthermore, Sears used the common concept for advancement of "getting to the next level" in many video games instead of traditional rating approaches to performance. Leaders in each category of performance are made visible and recognized with performance badges on this nationwide platform.

The impact of the performance gaming platform was significantly enhanced when Sears layered it on top of its proprietary in-house social network platform. Performance badges earned through the gaming system are added to employees' avatars in the social network for friends and colleagues to see. Sears's Chief Human Resources Officer Dean Carter said, "Sears has been able to boost our employee engagement and adherence to our goals as participation has dramatically increased. Instantly, hundreds of thousands of associates can see, learn, and send shout-outs nationally to our top performers. Through onsite blogs and storytelling, the game keeps growing in impact and 'stickiness.'"[5]

Knowledge is power when it comes to adherence. Understanding what is happening on your team empowers you to make adjustments to continually build competence and stay on the winning track. Start by balancing your view and keeping the score visible for all to see.

Chapter At-a-Glance

- **Balance your view**
  - Seek both dashboard (general) and under-the-hood (detailed) knowledge about your operation.
  - Track leading and lagging indicators.
  - Keep the score visible with a clear and compelling scoreboard.

If a man empties his purse into his head
no one can take it away from him.
An investment in knowledge always pays the best interest.

BENJAMIN FRANKLIN,
INVENTOR, AUTHOR, SCIENTIST,
AND STATESMAN

14

Boost Accountability with Specifics

ccountability means answering or accounting for your actions and results. It is something every leader wants more of from his or her team. Accountability is like rain—everyone knows they need it, but no one wants to get wet. It's easy to talk about how "they" need to be more accountable, but it can be uncomfortable when we apply it to ourselves. When is the last time you heard someone say, "I really need to be more accountable for my results?" It doesn't happen very often. Yet we get more accountability from our teams by being accountable to them. It's a two-way street.

Although almost every organization we have worked with struggles to some extent with accountability, retailers tend to do a better job of boosting accountability than most. A primary reason is the specificity of their performance metrics and expectations. Mike Barnes is a client and Group CEO for Signet Jewelers, a retail jeweler in the United States and United Kingdom operating 1,900 stores with 18,000 employees under the names Kay Jewelers, Jared the Galleria of Jewelry, J.B. Robinson, and H. Samuel, to name just a few. Barnes expressed his perspective on accountability this way: "We have to own our performance every day regardless of any 'noise' that might surround that performance. I think of the phrase, 'Don't talk to me about the storm; just bring in the ships.' We have to have personal and joint accountability for our performance, whether it's great or not, even when we feel that circumstances out of our control affected the performance."[1] The bottom line is that accountability means letting your actions rise above your excuses.

At its core, accountability is really about specificity—specific expectations, specific consequences, and specific language. Take a moment now to reflect on the performance of each team member. Think of the lowest-performing team member. By default, that person's level of performance sets the standard for acceptable performance on your team—it's the performance level that you as the leader allow. It's a very public and visible standard regardless of how much we might want to sweep it under the rug or turn a blind eye to it. Winning leaders realize that they owe it to their team to always raise that standard, and it can be done by getting specific. **Ambiguity is the Achilles' heel of accountability, but specificity enables you to raise the standards of your team's performance.**

Specific Expectations

Accountability starts at the beginning of the performance process. If we wait until the end, then we are simply imposing consequences rather than creating ownership. Therefore, crystal-clear expectations are the foundation for boosting accountability. **Blurry expectations lead to blurry results.** Leaders and team members should be able to easily agree on the answer to this question: "How will I know if I have met expectations?" We cannot rely on others' perceptions of our expectations. The imperfect nature of human communication requires us to be more specific than we think we need to be.

Winning teams hold themselves accountable for measurable improvements and for hitting milestones. To do this, accountable leaders help their teams by clearly and specifically defining the actions, timing, and results they expect from others and from themselves. For each member of your team, make certain you communicate:

- **Actions:** What steps need to be taken?
- **Timing:** By when? Be specific about when you want results—"next month" or "by second quarter" is not specific enough.

- **Results:** How will you (and they) know when the goal is achieved? Once you know what result you are trying to achieve, you can determine whether you are measuring quality, quantity, cost, or timeliness of your (and their) performance.

Although defining clear expectations can be tedious, if you take the necessary time to do it, you will end up spending less time dealing with performance problems and more time executing your plan. A broad and persuasive series of studies confirms that specificity of goals dramatically increases the likelihood of success. In one study, participants were asked to write a report on how they spent Christmas Eve and to write that report within two days after Christmas Eve. Half the participants were required to specify when and where within those two days they intended to write the report. The other half was not required to give specifics. Among those who had to provide specifics, 71 percent handed the reports in on time. Only 32 percent of the second group did so.[2]

In a business context, Stephen Mansfield, CEO of Methodist Health System in Dallas, has a handy technique to keep him and his team focused and accountable. Mansfield says, "I have a little handwritten index card for each direct report. On that card I write the three primary things that each person and I have agreed that I most need from them. I check in with each person every few weeks to ask how they are doing on those items. I always end the discussion with, 'Is there anything I can do to help?' I also use the opportunity to offer a pat on the back."[3] Mansfield is a master at applying the concept of proactive accountability—managing to specific expectations on the front end to boost accountability for results on the back end.

Paul Spiegelman is a client and CEO of The Beryl Companies. They partner with hospitals to enhance the patient experience in various service functions. Spiegelman hit on a subtle yet critical distinction when we discussed the timing aspect of expectations. He has found an unusual balance between accountability and the award-winning culture he has stewarded over the past 10 years at his booming company.

Spiegelman explains, "We don't like surprises. It's okay to give a leader a heads-up—that shows you are managing to timelines. But if you don't give a heads-up and you miss the deadline, then you are just managing to deadlines."[4] Henry Evans, author of *Winning with Accountability*, explains the difference between timelines and deadlines: "In school, most of us were taught about deadlines, which is 'when the work is due,' and we received very little training on timelines, which is 'when the work gets done.'"[5] When you help your team manage to specific timelines, you can prevent those tough discussions about missed deadlines.

Accountability Tracker
www.theLgroup.com/StickwithIt

Specific Consequences

To boost accountability, broaden your definition of consequences. We tend to think of consequences with respect to the short term—the immediate impact of our performance (positive or negative). That's the easy part of defining specific consequences. But it still leaves a lot to the imagination. As the circle of consequences below illustrates, we need to help employees see and understand the longer term, the downstream impact of their performances on team results, on the organization, on customers, on shareholders, and ultimately on themselves.

When employees see how their actions help or hinder each of their various constituents, the personal consequences of their performances become evident. External performance is ultimately a reflection of internal commitment. The personal impact on an employee might include opportunities for more (or fewer if the performance is substandard) promotions, development opportunities, exposure to executives, public

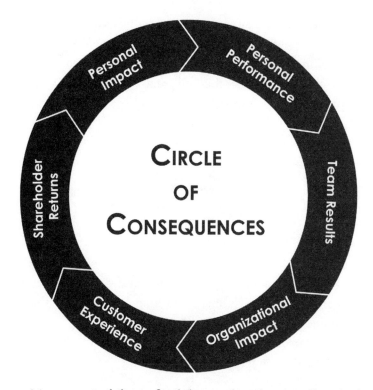

recognition, responsibilities, flexibility in the job, oversight of others, ownership of projects, and/or financial rewards. It is fair and appropriate to bring personal performance full circle back to these consequences. Our clients have found it useful to follow the circle of consequences with respect to their own leadership behaviors, particularly when they face tough situations. It illuminates the impact of their actions (or lack thereof) on various constituents and usually moves them from choosing avoidance to choosing courage.

Even on the most productive teams, there will be instances in which we have to muster leadership courage to address performance problems and ensure appropriate consequences. Earlier we mention Elaine Agather, head of J.P. Morgan Private Bank's South Region. She is a beloved and direct leader who understands the big picture of consequences as it relates to her role as a leader. Agather states, "The team is bigger than any issue at hand. The leader has a personal accountability to the team to have tough conversations and to occasionally make tough decisions with individuals."[6] Winning leaders such as Agather choose their team over personal discomfort. It reminds us of our son's former football coach, Chris Cunningham, who would preach this same leadership concept of "team over me" with this visual:

TEAM
me

As with expectations, when we specifically explain the consequences of individual performance up front, we minimize the tough conversations we need to have later on.

Specific Language

Even with clearly defined expectations and consequences, it's all too easy to let our accountability slip because of the language we use. **The power of our actions is preceded by the power of our words.** Speaking with specificity creates a sense of accountability and commitment. We can build accountability for others and ourselves by using specific phrases like these:

- Yes, I will do that for you.
- I'm not sure, but I'll give you a firm answer by noon tomorrow.
- I will own this.
- I will make time to get this done.
- I promise to close the loop by noon tomorrow so we can proceed.
- It will be done by Friday, March 18 at 2 p.m. Central.
- I will make it happen.

At the same time, we must replace "accountability killers" like the ones that follow because they sap energy and commitment from our teams:

- We'll see.
- I'll try.
- If I have the time.
- I will get back to you on that.
- Maybe.
- I'll do my best.
- When I get around to it.

Assess your own language of accountability by writing down the most common phrases or words you say and write in your communications. Take a moment now to write them here:

_____

_____

_____

Now, take a look at your language. Is it as specific as you want your team's language to be? Where can you be more specific? Do you use certain catch phrases that might not have specific and consistent meaning to others?

One of the classic lines from the movie *Star Wars: The Empire Strikes Back* was delivered by Yoda, the Jedi master: "Do, or do not. There is no try." If this 900-year-old little green guy can speak the language of accountability, so can we.

Accountability is a key driver of adherence. When everyone on the team is crystal clear about expectations and consequences and your language supports that, then adherence is enhanced.

Chapter At-a-Glance

- **Boost accountability with specifics**
  - Expectations—agree to actions, timing, and results.
  - Consequences—explain the circle of consequences.
  - Language—replace accountability killers with specific commitments.

You can't expect your employees to exceed the expectations
of your customers if you don't exceed
the employees' expectations of management.

HOWARD SCHULTZ
CEO, STARBUCKS

15

Building *Personal* Competence

Ebby Halliday is 101 years young and a business dynamo. She is the founder of the tenth largest real estate agency in the United States. Ebby Halliday Realtors and its team of over 1,400 sales associates and staff participate in more than 16,000 real estate transactions annually, exceeding sales of $3.5 billion. Ebby has been selling homes for more than 60 years. She started out selling hats for $10 a week (talk about building and rebuilding competence). Ebby was transferred from Kansas to Dallas in 1938 as manager of the ladies' hat department at the W. A. Green Department Store. Six years later she opened her own shop called Ebby's Hats. Her best customer was Virginia Murchison, wife of oil man and real estate developer Clint Murchison, Sr. Murchison had built concrete houses that looked fairly ugly. So he said to his wife, "The next time you visit your friend who sells the crazy hats, ask her if she has any ideas how I can sell my crazy houses."[1]

Ebby took the challenge, improved the concrete houses with carpet, curtains, and cottage furniture, and sold all of them within a year. She was inspired by this experience to enter the real estate business full time. Today, not only has she molded a premier real estate agency, but she also has shaped an industry—and she is still wheeling and dealing.

When you walk into Ebby's office, you are struck by the sheer number of accolades she has received. However, once you look beyond all the plaques, photos, letters, trophies, commendations, and even a Knights of the Round Table mounted sword, you see a relatively modest office. In one corner sits stacks of boxes. These boxes contain extra copies of books that Ebby has read and wants to share with others as gifts. It's a perfect metaphor for her life—Ebby has always been committed to learning, growing, and giving back. A self-described "voracious reader," she says she was influenced by the books she read from the shelves that were by the big stove in her one-room schoolhouse. Ebby knows that a reader is a leader, and a learner becomes an earner. Even with a century behind her, Ebby is still reading, learning, changing, exploring. In other words, she is still building her competence. Ebby truly is better than ever.

Ebby's long life of success and service offers rich lessons for each of us. She has not only built her own competence, but Ebby has very generously supported organizations that focus on building others' competence. Ebby's dream was never to just sell houses but to positively influence people's lives. And that she did—and still does.

Competence Actions

Following are some actions that highly successful people such as Ebby Halliday have taken to build their competence. Put a check mark next to the actions you already execute with excellence.

__ **Make the most of your natural gifts.**

Don't paint stripes on your back if you are not a zebra. Build upon your inherent strengths—your unique abilities. Then use your resourcefulness to minimize or eliminate your weaknesses.

__ **Seek feedback about your performance.**

Building competence requires courage—courage to face the facts. Be ready for what you might hear, and be prepared to make changes that might feel uncomfortable but that will build your competence.

— Team up with a mentor or coach.

Find someone who has a vested interest in your success and will tell you the unfiltered truth. This can be a boss, a colleague, or some other influential person in your life.

— Read to lead.

Keep a book or reading file with you to turn waiting time into learning time. Read or listen to one book per month, and you will be in the top 1 percent of all readers. (That's about half a chapter each day.) One book per month over 10 years comes to 120 books. Imagine the competence you can build with that kind of knowledge.

— Teach to learn.

Mentor and coach others whenever you can. As the proverb says, "In teaching others, we teach ourselves." Your teaching will deepen your own learning.

— Create it once; use it many times.

If you know you will perform a task more than once, create a checklist, form, or template to save time and improve your consistency over the long haul. No need to reinvent the wheel every time you coordinate an offsite meeting, prepare a proposal, send out a mailing, plan a new project timeline, or whatever.

— Escape from your comfort zone.

Try something new, visit a new place, or learn a new skill before you are forced to. Although our desire for comfort makes this challenging, it is always more effective and less painful to initiate change on our own terms. Remember, it takes more energy to resist change than to embrace it.

Close the Gap

Start closing the knowing-doing gap by reviewing the actions above and the at-a-glance summary below. Then, write down:

- One action you can take today to build your *team* competence

_____

_____

- One action you can take today to build your *personal* competence

_____

_____

COMPETENCE At-a-Glance

- **Treasure your talent**
  - Select smart—use the 3 x 3 x 3 interview process.
  - Treat employee development as a perpetual priority.
  - Coach for success with four steps: explain, ask, involve, and appreciate.

- **Get systematic**
  - Create repeatable work systems.
  - Collaborate with clear roles.
  - Innovate daily—what's the small idea?

- **Balance your view**
  - Seek both dashboard (general) and under-the-hood (detailed) knowledge about your operation.
  - Track leading and lagging indicators.
  - Keep the score visible with a clear and compelling scoreboard.

- **Boost accountability with specifics**
  - Expectations—agree to actions, timing, and results.
  - Consequences—explain the circle of consequences.
  - Language—replace accountability killers with specific commitments.

PART IV

Passion

Focus x **Competence** x **Passion** = *ADHERENCE*

During our recent trip to Italy that we previously mentioned, it was hard not to be awestruck by the great works we saw: The David sculpture, St. Peter's Basilica, the Sistine Chapel, the Roman Colosseum, and the Pantheon. What makes them great works? They were inspired and are lasting. In fact, our son asked, "What are we building today that will still be around in 2,000 years?" We were hard-pressed to give him a good answer.

This got us thinking about our most successful clients. They all inspire great work from their organizations by connecting daily tasks to something bigger than any one person on the team. They build a bridge between today's tasks and a better, brighter tomorrow. That bridge might be constructed of an inspiring vision, a deep sense of purpose to make a difference in the world, or their core values. These same clients take the long view. They want to build something lasting, and they make decisions knowing that they are in this for the long haul. In other words, they are building a cathedral for the ages, not a temporary temple.

To determine if you are building an inspired and lasting organization, just ask your team members what their jobs are. What would they say? What of significance do they see themselves building or providing as a service? Do they have passion for what they do and for what the organization does?

Although focus and competence are critical to adherence, passion is the glue that helps teams stick with their plans over the long term to create great work. Passion enables your team to turn stumbling blocks into stepping-stones. **The bookends of adherence are initiative and follow-through, and passion ignites them.** Passion provides the energy and the motivation to prevail. It is the intangible component that explains why some people and teams are able to adhere to their plans while other, equally talented people and teams are not. But let's not be Pollyannaish about passion. We should not expect every team member to be on fire about our goals. Our job as leaders is to help each team member ignite the maximum level of passion within his or her natural limits. "We believe a leader's job in developing people is not to put in what God left out but to draw out what God left in."

The passion component of the adherence equation is rooted in connections—connections to a deep sense of meaning for work, connections to fellow teammates, and connections to a sense of value and contribution. These connections meet the human needs for purpose, appreciation, and intimacy, which form the basis of emotional employee engagement that Lee describes in his book, *Engaging the Hearts and Minds of All Your Employees*.[1] Emotional engagement ignites passion.

The topic of employee engagement has been covered thoroughly in other books and warrants a full book to do it justice. For our purposes of illustrating the dynamics of adherence, consider a meta-analysis (i.e., an analysis of multiple related studies) in which researchers studied 32,394 business/work units composed of 955,905 employees. The researchers found that employee engagement is related to nine different business outcomes, including customer loyalty/engagement, profitability, productivity, turnover, safety incidents, shrinkage, absenteeism, patient safety incidents, and quality (defects).[2] The bottom line is that when we fully engage our team, we ignite the passion that drives positive business results. The seemingly intangible component of the adherence equation—passion—yields very tangible results.

Passion drives engagement because it answers the "why" question—why is executing your strategy important to the organization and meaningful for your team? **A team without passion is a team without purpose.** Team passion ignites mental toughness that enables employees to see opportunities that otherwise might be seen as obstacles. Passion also elicits discretionary effort and a willingness to sacrifice for the greater purpose.

Leverage these four adherence accelerators to ignite your team's passion:

1. Paint the picture of a larger purpose for your team to give daily activities meaning.
2. Give what you want. We all want respect and appreciation, so we must give it to our teams.
3. Value your values by incorporating them in your decision-making process and in guiding your actions.
4. Create connections with rituals and accessibility.

Let's look at each of these four adherence accelerators further.

Years may wrinkle the skin,
but to give up enthusiasm wrinkles the soul."

Samuel Ullman, Poet

16

Paint the Picture

We have discussed sharpening focus and building competence. These are the things that capture employees' minds. To capture their hearts and ignite their passion, you must meet one of their most basic psychological needs—the need to contribute to something bigger, to paint the picture of the deeper purpose behind their jobs.

Cheryl Johnson is a client and a corporate leader with Ulta Beauty, a rapidly growing retailer of beauty products and services. During one particular discussion, we talked about how painting the picture can ignite a passion for people to go the extra mile. Cheryl was reflecting on one of her first jobs as a dishwasher in a hospital. Interestingly, she didn't see her job as that of only a dishwasher. Most people would wallow in the mundane task of washing dishes, but Cheryl's boss painted a picture of something much more significant. On the first day of work, her boss told Cheryl that her job was "to help ensure a clean, healthy environment so patients could heal as fast as possible and go home to their families." Wouldn't you be more passionate about washing dishes if that was your purpose?

We often hear the adage, "Make every minute count!" But count toward what? How do we know if our minutes count? We have to measure our time and our efforts against something. That something is our purpose. Without a compelling purpose, we are just putting in time. Our minds might be engaged, but our hearts will not be. The work world offers great opportunities for people to connect with a bigger purpose. If you want your team members to make every minute count, give them something to be passionate about. When you get your team members inspired about a purpose, their hearts will follow.

The Fundamental Four

Our purpose answers the most fundamental question, "Why do we do what we do?" If your organization has a stated purpose, connect your team's work directly to it. If no one has yet painted the organizational picture, don't wait. Take the initiative to define a purpose for your team. Step back and look at the big picture. Consider how your team members improve conditions for others—what differences do they make? Be bold. Your team's purpose should stir emotions. At the same time, keep your purpose real and relevant because people can commit only to what they understand.

Then, in order to paint the picture of that purpose, you must answer the fundamental four questions that every employee asks (whether or not they ask them aloud):

1. Where are we going?
2. What are we doing to get there?
3. How can I contribute?
4. What's in it for me?

Like all aspects of leadership and adherence, painting the picture is not accidental. Our clients who paint a clear picture for their teams are intentional about answering the fundamental four questions. Some of them even use the questions as a checklist to ensure that the content of significant communiqués addresses each question. As a result, the passion in their organizations is palpably higher and their results are greater.

Answering the fundamental four creates a bridge that connects today's tasks to the broader team or organizational purpose. Without purpose, team members may achieve short-term results, but they won't have the heart to go the distance. On the other hand, they naturally will be more passionate about their work and more motivated to stick with the plan when they clearly understand that they are part of something bigger.

Silence Spiral

Every day, with every interaction, we are painting the picture with our team. The picture is never complete—we have to continuously answer the fundamental four questions. With today's information-overloaded workplace, it can be challenging to decide what to communicate to employees and what to withhold. It's easy to say (usually to ourselves), "They don't really need to know all that," or, "My team won't really understand," or, "I don't think they can handle that news right now." But the truth is that when we *under*estimate the intelligence of others, we also tend to *over*estimate our own.

When employees don't get the information they need, including the answers to the fundamental four questions, they tend to fill in the blanks with their own assumptions, and their assumptions are often worst-case scenarios. This is not necessarily a reflection on their leader. It's our natural human insecurity. We often assume the worst in the absence of evidence to the contrary. Lack of information and unanswered questions can start the *silence spiral*:

Silence leads to doubt ⇒
    Doubt leads to fear ⇒
        Fear leads to panic ⇒
            Panic leads to worst-case thinking.

The silence spiral undermines trust and puts a damper on passion. It can take five minutes or five weeks to play out, but in most cases, it happens more rapidly than we would imagine. A closed office door, a vague reply to an honest question, an unreciprocated greeting as you pass in the hallway, or a cancelled one-on-one meeting without explanation can all trigger the silence spiral. Even if these actions take place with good reason, if they are not the norm, it can be enough to open the door of doubt in our minds and start the silence spiral.

We recall a situation in which the silence spiral spun out of control in a public setting. A local company was required to make costly aesthetic improvements to the grounds of its corporate campus to avoid even more costly fines for not being in compliance with the city's landscaping ordinance. Although these improvements had been planned for over six months, unfortunately, work began the very day the company announced a reduction in force at its headquarters. This caused both terminated and surviving employees to be extremely disillusioned. The company never told employees the improvements were required by a city ordinance, carried substantial fines for noncompliance, and had been planned for six months. In the silence of no communication, people typically assume the worst. In this case, they assumed the the company's leadership was intentionally adding insult to injury by spending money on landscaping instead of its employees. This resulted in negative publicity from terminated employees and in significantly reduced commitment from surviving employees. Even though the company's home-office landscaping had nothing to do with its strategy, the silence spiral had a direct, negative impact on employees' passion, discretionary effort, and adherence to the company's plan.

Prevent the silence spiral by proactively painting the picture. Nothing compares to hearing the facts directly from the boss. For example, if you learn about a new project that won't affect your team for a few months, go ahead and tell the team members about it now. They can start preparing, or at minimum, they won't be caught off guard or be inclined to listen to and perpetuate rumors. Winning leaders realize that they are not really protecting their teams by keeping them in the dark. They know that their employees will either find out on their own or may make assumptions that are worse than reality. More important, silence chips away at trust. So use every interaction, meeting, and communiqué as an opportunity to paint a vivid picture for your team.

Chapter At-a-Glance

- **Paint the picture**
  - Connect each job to a broader purpose.
  - Always answer the fundamental four questions.
  - Communicate proactively to avoid the silence spiral.

In a knowledge economy, a good business is a community with a purpose, not a piece of property.

CHARLES HANDY, MANAGEMENT
EXPERT AND AUTHOR

17

Give What You Want

If you want passion from your team, you have to give it. Think about your interactions with others. Are they filled with enthusiasm and energy, or are they flat and lifeless? Your level of passion is reflected back to you—it's your boomerang to the world. This is another example of the inside-out approach to leadership. When it comes to passion, you have to start with yourself. **Give what you want, and you will get what you need.**

This principle also holds true when it comes to how we treat team members. Every employee (and human being for that matter) wants respect, appreciation, and encouragement. Contrary to popular belief, most employees do not quit their jobs because of compensation issues or something "the company" did. Employees typically quit because of how they are treated by their direct supervisor. People quit people, not companies. And it often comes down to a simple matter of respect and appreciation. Sometimes we forget that it's the little things that make the most difference. Treating team members with respect and appreciation, and offering them encouragement along the way, provides the initial spark of passion.

Show Respect

We all want to be treated with decency and respect. Unfortunately, in today's fast-paced work world, showing common respect has become an uncommon practice. The best way to *get* respect is to *give it* first.

It boils down to using good manners. Talk about the knowing-doing gap! We all know what good manners entail. Showing respect for others includes demonstrating those behaviors we all learned as kids: smiling, saying "please" and "thank you," using employees' names when talking with them, and respecting others' time and talents. This sounds like a list that should be posted on a kindergarten classroom wall; but we frequently forget these common courtesies.

Here are some other simple ways to show uncommon respect with common courtesies:

- Silence your cell phone when you're in meetings.
- Keep eye contact during conversations.
- Address performance issues in private.
- Greet people before talking business.
- Show up for meetings on time.
- Ask others if they have time to talk before jumping into a discussion.
- Converse with people instead of lecturing them.
- Maintain emotional control.
- If you were wrong, just say so.

Sometimes, in the midst of the daily challenges life throws at us, we miss what is really important. We may fail to say hello, congratulate someone on something wonderful that has happened, give a compliment, or just do something nice for no particular reason. We can show respect by learning about who our team members are as people (family, outside interests, etc.) and acknowledging them as human beings. These simple behaviors deepen respect and lay the foundation for passionate performance.

Demonstrate Appreciation

William James the father of psychology stated that the most fundamental psychological need is to be appreciated. We want to feel fully appreciated for our work. Unfortunately, the reality is that lack of appreciation is the number one reason people leave their jobs. The direct supervisor is the primary source of appreciation (or lack thereof), the primary influencer of job satisfaction and engagement, and as we said earlier, the primary reason people either leave or stay on the job.

Showing appreciation is a common blind spot for leaders—and for people in any relationship for that matter. We feel appreciative of those at work and at home who are important to us. Yet if we were to ask those people to rate how much they feel appreciated, more than likely it would be lower than our rating of how much we appreciate them. Why is that? The reason for this disconnect is that we don't often enough convert our thoughts of appreciation into visible acts of appreciation. While we judge ourselves by our intentions, others judge us by our actions. That's why we used the word "demonstrate" in the heading for this section. What is important is not how much we appreciate people but rather how much we *demonstrate* that appreciation (again, the knowing-doing gap). **Demonstrating appreciation is not a matter of time and intention; it is a matter of priority and action.**

A survey of 15 million people worldwide illuminates the business benefits of appreciation. This Gallup study by Tom Rath and Donald Clifton found that people who receive regular recognition at work:

- Experience increased productivity.
- Enjoy increased engagement with colleagues.
- Are more likely to stay with the organization.
- Receive higher loyalty and satisfaction scores from customers.
- Have better safety records and fewer accidents on the job.[1]

Appreciation comes down to basic psychology—reinforce those behaviors that you want to see more frequently. Look for opportunities to recognize and appreciate your team's efforts and results. When you catch team members doing something right, acknowledge it—and do it often. As Rath and Clifton say in their book, *How Full Is Your*

Bucket, "Shine a light on what is right." Thinking back to the yellow car phenomenon, if you look for positive performance you will find plenty of instances to appreciate.

The good news is that you have complete control over your appreciation. No budget limitations or excuses here—there are literally thousands of ways to demonstrate your appreciation at little or no cost. You can occasionally offer a gift card or something of modest value, but you should rely more on your creativity and knowledge of the employee to personalize your appreciation so that it is meaningful. The key to appreciation is making it sincere and specific. Don't fall into the trap of blurting out the robotic, "Good job." Take the time to explain why you appreciate an employee's performance, such as "I really appreciate the way you kept our customer happy without incurring more cost."

In our work at client organizations, we have seen more than a few handwritten notes of appreciation on employees' desks. Often these cards are several years old (up to five years in one case), yet are still prominently and proudly displayed. We often wonder if the bosses who wrote them understood how much discretionary effort their three-minute investment yielded or knew how meaningful those cards were to the employees who received them. Greg Brown, senior vice president of enterprise operations at The Hartford, says, "The little things you do are more important than the big things you say." Brown sends handwritten anniversary cards and electronic birthday cards to each of his approximately 1,100 leaders. He makes a habit of writing notes to anyone he catches doing something right. By the way, his CEO does the same things.[2]

Find a way to express your appreciation that is natural to you. Not everyone is a note/card writer, but every leader has a way of showing appreciation that feels authentic. As long as your appreciation is specific and sincere, you don't need to worry about going overboard. In fact, there are no documented studies of employees ever feeling *over*appreciated! So the sky is the limit. Remember, **we do more for those who appreciate us.**

To ignite passion, we must not only appreciate good performance but also appreciate the person. It is easy to appreciate the top performers who bail you out of tight spots or whose hard work makes you look good. It is more challenging, but more meaningful, to appreciate the person, regardless of performance. Can you appreciate employees' reliability, their service to others outside of work, their consistently professional demeanor or attire, their integrity in gray situations, their willingness to coach new team members, their optimistic outlook, or their ability to keep personal challenges at home and remain focused on the job? Appreciating the person engages the heart.

Let's take a look at Charles Plumb's life and learn a lesson about appreciating the person.

Charles Plumb was a U.S. Navy pilot in Vietnam. After 75 combat missions, his plane was shot down. He ejected and parachuted into enemy hands. He was captured and spent six years in a Vietnamese prison. He survived the ordeal and now lectures on the lessons learned from that experience.

One day, Plumb and his wife were sitting in a restaurant when a man came up and said, "You're Plumb! You flew jet fighters in Vietnam from the aircraft carrier *Kitty Hawk*. You were shot down!"

"How in the world did you know that?" asked Plumb.

"I packed your parachute," the man replied. Plumb gasped in surprise and gratitude. The man pumped his hand and said, "I guess it worked!"

Plumb assured him, "It sure did. If that chute hadn't worked, I wouldn't be here today."

Plumb couldn't sleep that night, thinking about the man. He thought of the many hours the sailor had spent on a long wooden table in the bowels of the ship—carefully folding the silks of each chute, holding someone's fate in his hands.

Plumb later said, "I kept wondering what he might have looked like in a navy uniform—white hat, bib in the back, bell-bottom trousers. I wondered how many times I might have seen him and not even said, 'Good morning, how are you?' because, you see, I was a fighter pilot and he was just a sailor."[3]

We all have someone who provides what we need to make us more productive. Focus on the people, not titles. Remember, at the end of the day, your success is based more on what your people do than what you do. So ask yourself, "Who is packing my parachute?"

Three Words to Encourage

Some people literally change the world for good—people like Gandhi, Mother Teresa, Abraham Lincoln, and Thomas Edison. Although it's an ambitious goal to change the world, we often underestimate our singular power to positively change the world of those around us. Each of us has the power to change someone's world with the gift of encouragement. We don't even have to *do* anything! We only have to say three simple words. Try one of these three-word, power-packed statements to change a team member's world:

- I appreciate you.
- You are terrific.
- I trust you.
- I promise you. (Then keep the promise)
- Take a chance.
- You will succeed.

Whether it's a long conversation with an employee, colleague, boss, friend, or relative, or simply placing an order at a restaurant, every word makes a difference. The results of our interactions are rarely neutral; they are almost always positive or negative. Ask yourself, "Do my words reflect my passion to encourage others, create win-wins, continuously learn, embrace change, and support my team's success?"

Positive, encouraging words are the seeds of commitment. Once they are spoken, they grow into results. Whether those results become apparent sooner or later (like the bamboo seed), when we speak words of encouragement, we can expect victory. Plant the seeds of success in someone's mind and heart today. You'll start a positive ripple effect that will be felt by many people and many miles away, not to mention the positive effect you will feel inside.

Show respect, demonstrate appreciation, and encourage others. These simple actions will ignite a powerful passion in your team. Remember, give what you want, and you will get what you need.

Chapter At-a-Glance

- **Give what you want**
  - Show uncommon respect with common courtesy.
  - Appreciate performance as well as the person behind it.
  - Encourage others with three simple words.

---

*People don't care how much you know until
they know how much you care.*

John C. Maxwell, Leadership
Expert and Author

18

Value Your Values

A few years ago, we built and moved into our dream home. We had spent years planning and designing every aspect and detail of the house. Throughout the long but worthwhile process, we discovered that leadership corresponds to the phases of home building. Constructing a house occurs in three major stages: foundation, framing, and finish out.

The first stage is setting the foundation. Once our builder poured the foundation, we were committed to a certain floor plan and the way the house would flow. We chose to take extra measures to ensure that we had a solid foundation, knowing that any movement could cause cracks in the future that would be difficult and expensive to repair. Building a team, like building a house, starts with a solid foundation. A team's foundation is its values. Once the values are set, they determine how the team will flow and how team members will interact with one another. A strong foundation helps prevent cracks in the team and ensures smooth interactions, sound decisions, and predictable results.

The next phase is framing. The builder erects wood studs on top of the foundation and then installs all the plumbing pipes and miles of electrical wiring between the studs. These form the "guts" of the home operating systems—climate control, water, lighting, television, Internet access, security, stereo, and all appliances. For the team builder, framing defines the systems and processes for getting work done.

These mechanisms include goal setting, training, decision making, task prioritization, communication, quality assurance, customer service, and problem solving.

The final stage is finish out. This is when the builder paints, lays carpet, plants the landscaping, and installs lighting fixtures, appliances, and countertops. Finish out adds the final touches that make a house personal and unique. In "finishing out" a team, the team builder paints the picture of the team's purpose, plants the seeds of productive relationships, and installs rituals (covered in the next chapter). The seasoned team builder allows team members to add their own finishing touches to create a special and unique team culture and to build a sense of long-term job ownership.

Regardless of the quality of the framing and finish out, a house—or any building, for that matter—is only as strong as its foundation. The Tower of Pisa in Italy, for example, leans about 17 feet from perpendicular because it was built on an inadequate foundation—a mere three meters, set in weak, unstable subsoil. Foundation problems can be difficult to detect, and our tendency is to fix the "symptom" rather than the root cause. We see a crack in a floor tile, so we replace the tile. A bedroom door doesn't swing quite right, so we adjust the hinges. A window doesn't close flush, so we caulk the bottom to seal the gap.

As with a building, **a team is only as strong as the foundational values on which it is built.** And just as in a home, cracks in a team's foundation can be difficult to spot. Problems with a team's foundational values can initially look like a simple framing or finish-out problem. If we find ourselves repeatedly dealing with the same issues on our team, they are likely symptoms of a deeper crack in our foundational values. For instance, we might observe an increase in product errors coming from our team, so we provide additional training and more detailed work procedures to reduce the error rate. However, if the root of the problem exists in our foundation—perhaps a lack of mutual trust among team members—we can tinker all day with our team's framing and finish out without improving results. Similarly, what looks like an innocent crack in the wall (e.g., a blip in employee turnover) could actually indicate a deeper problem in our foundation (e.g., a disconnect between our values and our actions).

Winning leaders know they must first pour a strong foundation of values before they can build a house to lead in. Then they frame and finish out their teams by converting values to behaviors and making values-based decisions.

Values to Behaviors

Strongly held values create a strong team foundation. However, most values such as respect, teamwork, innovation, excellence, and customer focus are just concepts, and it's difficult to measure and manage concepts. **Only by converting our values into behaviors can we measure and manage them.** That's how we bring our values to life—by describing and modeling behaviors that demonstrate each value. This helps everyone understand the intended spirit of the values, minimizes misinterpretations, and defines observable behaviors for which the team is held accountable. Then our stated values are aligned with our operating values, and we are working with integrity. Values in action are the glue to a winning culture.

Defining specific, behavioral examples helps clarify the intention of each value. For instance, a team value of "service excellence" can be interpreted many ways: Is the customer always right? Do we provide excellent service at any cost? Do we serve external customers before internal customers? Are inquiries answered within an hour, a day, or a week? One of our favorite behaviors for the value of customer service comes from Sharon Goldstein who is the campus operating officer of Berkley College Online. Her team lives by the mantra, "I am my customer!" and constantly asks, "How would I feel if I listened to the voice message I just left or read the e-mail I just sent?"[1] These questions help keep their actions aligned with their value of customer service. It's a wonderfully simple and powerful way to create self-accountability for great service.

Converting Values to Behaviors

Value	Definition	Team Commitment	Indicators	Examples
Integrity	We are personally and professionally responsible to each other, our donors, and volunteers, fostering an environment of trust and setting the standard for accountability in our industry.	I am responsible for my actions.	• Disclose misconduct to the appropriate personnel. • Owns mistakes. • Keeps Promises and obligations. • Takes ownership of a task to its completion. • Honors company policies and ethics at all times. • Asks questions when unsure about areas of responsibility.	Tom in sales raised a minor, potential conflict-of-interest issue with our biggest prospect, knowing it might take us out of consideration for the new business.
Teamwork	Through collaboration and teamwork, with internal and external partners, we generate the greatest impact on health and human service needs in our communities.	I will collaborate with others to achieve goals.	• Understands other departmental processes, procedures, and skills. • Takes advantage of available opportunities to understand how other departments function. • Supports the needs of internal and external partners in a timely manner. • Maintains open communication with internal and external partners.	Sara in finance initiated a ride-along with a colleague in sales in order to better understand his process so she could help resolve a problem they were having reconciling sales bids with actual invoices.

If you really want your values to stick with your team, involve team members in the process of clarifying the values. People are committed to what they help create, so let them interpret the values and define behaviors (within your acceptable boundaries). You can facilitate this by asking questions like:

- What do our team values mean to you?
- How do these values make you feel?
- What specific behaviors do you think best demonstrate these values?
- What could you do differently to better reflect these values in your work?

We find that our clients' employees create more specific and more meaningful behavioral examples of values than their leaders would have on their own. Below is an online link to a sample values-to-behaviors worksheet that we use with our clients in collaboration with their employees.

Converting Values to Behaviors Worksheet
www.theLgroup.com/StickwithIt

If our values are to become more than just a plaque on the wall, team members must perceive them as meaningful and live them daily. Our actions and our words are good indicators of our true beliefs and values. Here is a quick exercise you can do right now to get an indication of your team's operating values (regardless of the stated values). Write down five common phrases that are spoken and written by your team. (For example: "I need to get approval." "We don't have the budget." "I need it ASAP." "Just do it." "Collaborate." "Show me the data." "Where's the report?" "I'll do my best." "We need to have a meeting." "Let's hustle." "We tried that already.")

1. _____
2. _____
3. _____
4. _____
5. _____

What do your words tell you about your team values? Think about what each phrase (or combination of phrases) might indicate. If you frequently hear, "Let's find a win-win," it could say something about how you value teamwork. On the other hand, if you hear, "That's not my responsibility," it might reflect silo thinking and lack of team focus. Whatever words you wrote, they say something (although not necessarily everything) about your values.

Your team values create an important, emotional connection for employees. The key to developing passion is to convert those values into observable behaviors and allow team members to personalize the values as their own.

Values-Based Decisions

Benjamin Franklin addressed values-based decisions years ago when he said, "We stand at a crossroads, each minute, each hour, each day, making choices. We choose the thoughts we allow ourselves to think, the passions we allow ourselves to feel, and the actions we allow ourselves to perform. Each choice is made in the context of whatever values system we have selected to govern our lives. In selecting that values system, we are in a very real way, making the most important choice we will ever make."

Over the years, we have seen hundreds of sets of organizational and team values plastered on every imaginable surface. All too often though, those values are not embedded into daily work and decisions. It's easy to spot values-driven organizations by observing their decision-making process. Rarely a day goes by without a decision being made that explicitly considers one of their values.

We partnered with Barry Davis, CEO of Crosstex Energy Services, while the business was still in its infancy, to help develop its foundational E4 values: excellence, employee focus, ethics, and enthusiasm. His team articulated actionable descriptors to support each value. Today, Crosstex is a billion-dollar enterprise, and the E4 values have been the core of its culture during the past 16 years of growth. Even as the company quintupled in head count and locations, Crosstex continued to conduct all-employee quarterly meetings to demonstrate its value of employee focus. This decision came with significant time and financial investments. If Davis had based the return on investment (ROI) analysis solely on the numbers, he would have stopped the meetings a long time ago. But because he was committed to living the company's values, Davis and his team maintained the all-employee quarterly meetings as a forum for communication and for staying connected with the business and its people.[2]

Similarly, we recall a Fortune 1000 company that wanted to offer new employee benefits that would give employees more choices for meeting varying personal needs. But these new benefits came with a multimillion-dollar price tag. The board approved the plan based on the company's core value of "respect for the individual." Board members realized that the cost of not living their values was ultimately much greater than the cost of the new benefits.

If you don't use your values to make decisions and guide your actions, then why have them? If *you* do not value your team's values, no one else will. So, as you are faced with decisions, use your values to help you determine what to do. Making a values-based decision sends a strong message about your values and your leadership. Take the time to communicate your values, allow your team to personalize them, and, most important, live them. Taking these steps will ignite your team's passion, resulting in a willingness to go the extra mile and stick with your plan.

Chapter At-a-Glance

- **Value your values**
  - Build a solid foundation of values.
  - Define and manage behaviors that exemplify your values.
  - Make values-based decisions.

---

*It's not hard to make decisions
when you know what your values are.*

Roy Disney
Director Emeritus,
The Walt Disney Company

19

Create Connections

We often hear people speak with envy about companies with "real heart"—companies like Starbucks, Ben & Jerry's, Southwest Airlines, Harley-Davidson, Nordstrom, The Container Store, Apple, FedEx, and Google, to name a few. Outsiders are constantly looking for these companies' secrets to success. The "secret" is the connectedness within their teams. Their teams have strong connections that ignite strong passion that helps them adhere to their plans and deliver outstanding results.

Lest you think that "connectedness" refers to being technologically connected (which most of us are all day, every day), let us clarify. We are talking about connecting with other people in authentic ways. The fact is that **we live in a high-tech world, but creating real connections is still a high-touch job.** To illustrate the power of connections, consider an experiment regarding the effects of relationships on group performance. This experiment compared the performance of groups of three friends to groups of three acquaintances. Each group was asked to follow specific instructions for building models made with Tinkertoys. The friends built an average of 9.0 models compared to 2.45 models for the acquaintances. "[The friends] were able to challenge one another's ideas in a constructive way," said Karen Jehn, one of the researchers. "In the groups of acquaintants, people were almost too polite."[1]

So what is the learning here? Connections among teammates increase engagement and productivity. These findings have been validated by other studies that show that strong connections and bonds among employees also enhance loyalty, retention, and job satisfaction.[2] Indeed, connections are the "secret" of winning organizations. You can encourage and support the connections that form productive relationships and generate a great ROC (return on connections). You can reinforce rituals, be accessible to your employees, and be authentic with your team. Let's look at each of these in more detail.

Ritualize Your Team

College fraternities and sororities understand the power of rituals. They use rituals to make members feel connected to one another through unique yet common experiences (mostly legal experiences, hopefully). Their rituals include secret passwords and handshakes, special chants and songs, required activities, pregame tailgate parties, goofy antics for pledges, and time-honored initiation ceremonies. Their special rituals are the things they do together but are also different from what other fraternities and sororities do. As a result, they create strong and long-lasting personal connections.

Before you think that we are suggesting that you gather your team around a campfire and sing "Kumbaya," let us translate rituals into the business setting. First, every team has rituals, regardless of whether you recognize them as such. We have rituals around hiring, recognition, production, innovation, quality, promotions, family, customer service, community service, learning, and so on. To be clear, we are not advocating rituals for ritual's sake. They should be intentionally designed to meet a business need or the team's need for connection. Effective rituals fit your leadership style and the chemistry of your team—they feel natural. And they must be performed with 100 percent reliability. So if you celebrate team members' birthdays monthly on "last Friday birthdays," but you forgot to do it twice last year, then it's not a ritual. Effective rituals are reliable, expected, and reveled in by teams.

Here are a few ways you can ritualize your team (you likely are already doing some of these):

What do you want to reinforce?	Which rituals fit your leadership style and team culture?
Outstanding performance	• "Ring the bell" to announce success! • Pass a fun trophy to someone who has gone above and beyond (should be public and ceremonial). • Post photos of new customers outside the office(s)/cubicle(s) of the team member(s) who helped acquire them. • Take the "star" to lunch.
Productive relationships/teamwork	• Morning huddles to identify your "one thing" for that day (yes, meetings are a ritual). • Assign "buddies" to new team members. • Have a unique, fun way of introducing new team members. • Host last Friday brown bag lunches or first Monday donut/bagel days. • Make the rounds each morning to say "hello" to your team. • Say a team cheer. (This is not for everyone, but it is for Walmart. Employees yell each letter in the company name.)
Safety	• For every month in which there are no safety violations, hold a Friday afternoon "healthy hour" with snacks and drinks (nonalcoholic, of course).
Community service	• Organize a relay team for an annual weekend walk/run for a local cause. • Pack meals as a team at a local food bank once a quarter. • As a team, tutor children once a month at a local school.

Get intentional about your rituals. Start with the business or team needs, and then determine if you already have rituals in place that reinforce those needs. If you do, ensure that your team is 100 percent consistent with them (i.e., systematize them). Rituals that are well designed stand the test of time; but occasionally a ritual can become "stale" or no longer reinforces the need. In that case, change the elements that aren't working or replace the ritual with a new one. If you do not have a ritual in place, get creative and develop one that feels natural. Then systematize it so that it's easy to sustain. And finally, make sure to involve your team members—they are often the best source of ideas for rituals.

One of our favorite examples of rituals comes from a client who wanted to speed up the forming of connections within a new team. We suggested that the team leader incorporate a quick "high/low" around the group at the start of each meeting. Some of our clients call this ritual "peaks and pits." The team leader starts by stating one high (positive experience) and one low (negative experience) that took place since the last meeting. The highs and lows can be either personal or work related. Each person in the group does the same around the table. No long monologues here; the leader keeps things moving fast. For instance, a leader's high might be that her daughter just won a piano competition, and a low might be that a key player decided to leave the company. A team member's high could be that he hit last week's deadline and was under budget, while the low could be that his father was just diagnosed with cancer.

Since we started suggesting this short but powerful ritual to our clients, many have found it to be a valuable window into the world of their teams. It creates real-time opportunities to support team members who need help (like lending resources to get a project back on track or having dinner sent home during trying times). It also enables the leader to recognize them for positive contributions (such as the time they spent over the weekend serving the needy or going the extra mile to recover a customer who had left). The initial client who used this high/low ritual to help his team gel kept it as a permanent part of his meetings because he found it to be so valuable. Truth be told, so did his team.

Another favorite is from a client who creatively solved a short-term team need with a fun ritual. This leader needed shared knowledge of all job functions within his relatively small team to ensure that team members could provide uninterrupted service if one of them was sick, on vacation, or pulled away to help on a special project. So he used a game show format where each month, a different team member "quizzed" the other team members about their job duties and responsibilities. The leader made it a fun experience, and the person with the best score received a candy bar, just something small to stir their competitive juices. After six months, every team member had given his or her quiz, and the ritual had run its course. It met the business need of stimulating cross-functional conversation that continues today. As a result, his team can confidently ensure coverage every day throughout the year.

Rituals Worksheet
www.theLgroup.com/StickwithIt

Access and Authenticity

As we were writing this book, we asked lots of clients and colleagues questions about their experiences with adherence, including this one: What is the most critical action a senior leader can take to improve consistent adherence to a plan? We repeatedly received the same answer: Be accessible and be yourself. In other words, as leaders, our time and our authenticity are keys to igniting passion and sticking with our plans.

We recently saw a small, inspirational gift book that posed the question, "How does a child spell 'love'?" The book takes the reader through all the brief moments in a parent's life that are defining moments in a child's life. The moral of these moments is that a child spells "love" as t-i-m-e.[3] Your team spells it the same way. **Time is our most precious resource.** We cannot make more of it, and we all have the same amount of it each day, from the CEO to the frontline worker. It speaks volumes when we give our most precious resource to someone who needs it. Considering that we can achieve sustained adherence only through our team, what better place to invest our time than in creating connections?

One of our colleagues, who is a senior executive in the financial services industry, demonstrated her accessibility to a newly promoted manager. She considered this manager to be a high-potential individual who needed little of her time or supervision. As a result, she asked him to provide an update 90 days after his promotion to see how he was doing. Her request for a 90-day update turned into 90 daily updates! But that did not sway our colleague's confidence in her newly promoted manager. She patiently gave her full attention to him during each daily update because she recognized that her new manager simply wanted to ensure that they were in sync. She knew that her time was of great value to this budding leader, so she willingly gave it to him. Today, she gets only the 90-day updates she originally requested from this high performer.

Being accessible and giving our time is certainly an important step, but we must do it authentically in order for it to really ignite passion. **There is no room for putting on airs with today's workers.** They want and respond to "the real deal"—a real human being leading in the best way he or she knows how. We've all heard the phrase, "He really walks the talk." It's a statement about personal alignment—that a person's actions match his words. This principle is echoed in a Chrysler ad that says, "The strongest statements are made without saying a word." Living authentically creates a far greater positive impact than just talking about what you are going to do. While your team (and your children) will not always follow your words, they will naturally and predictably walk in your path. St. Francis of Assisi said, "Preach the gospel always. If necessary, use words." We are challenged to do the same in our leadership roles—to model the behaviors we expect from our teams.

We can demonstrate authentic leadership by working alongside our team rather than above them. Regardless of the size or scope of winning organizations, we find that top leaders are willing to roll up their sleeves and get to work. We mention Dave Feinberg, MD, earlier in the book. In his role as president of UCLA Health System, Feinberg spends two hours a day doing rounds, talking with patients, helping them get to the toilet, taking them for walks in their wheelchairs, asking them questions, and acknowledging mistakes (then correcting them). He even gives patients a business card with his cell phone number on it. Predictably, his entire leadership team models that practice.[4] How do you think his team, all the way down to the front line, responds to seeing this? How would your team respond? It is no coincidence that UCLA is a premier healthcare system and that its top leader is highly accessible and authentic.

To be clear, Feinberg will tell you that he is not perfect. But as a leader, he is who he is. In success or failure, he is the same person. That holds true for each of the clients and colleagues we have highlighted throughout this book. Winning leaders know who they are, know they are not perfect, and are comfortable with it. And that is precisely what makes their teams passionate about following them.

Chapter At-a-Glance

- **Create connections**
  - Ritualize your team.
  - Be accessible to your team.
  - Be who you are and nobody else.

People will forget what you said.
They will even forget what you did.
But they will never forget how you made them feel.

MAYA ANGELOU, POET

20

Igniting *Personal* Passion

Born in Ho Chi Minh City in 1967, Taryn Rose narrowly escaped Vietnam with her family three days before the fall of Saigon when she was just eight years old. In the midst of machine gun and artillery fire, she and her family boarded a plane that took them to Fort Smith, Arkansas. Eventually, the family moved to Southern California. After getting her undergraduate degree from the University of California at Irvine, she attended USC's medical school to become an orthopedic surgeon. (Her father was also a physician.) But soon after finishing her residency, she decided to stop following in her father's footsteps and to instead follow her own passion which did actually involve footsteps.

The 14-hour shifts that Dr. Rose often worked in high-fashion, high-heeled shoes played a significant part in her career move, but so did all of her female patients whose feet were in pain and in need of surgery because of the shoes they were wearing. A high-heel lover herself, Dr. Rose saw a need in the marketplace and an opportunity to combine her knowledge of foot biomechanics with her passion for fashion. So the surgeon became a shoe designer. She spent three years getting her namesake company off the ground, researching everything from accounting to manufacturing, developing a business plan, and obtaining a loan.

Fast-forward to today. Taryn Rose has created one of the most successful and highly coveted brands in footwear, carried at stores such as Neiman Marcus and Nordstrom. She married fashion and function and changed the footwear industry forever. Her idea of being well dressed with a sense of well-being connected with women from coast to coast, creating a dedicated following for her footwear collections. What started in her garage grew to a $40 million business.[1] One step at a time, Taryn Rose ignited her own passion to create a product that thousands of women are passionate about.

Passion Actions

Following are some actions that highly passionate people like Taryn Rose take. Put a check mark next to the actions you already execute with excellence.

__ **Be fearless.**

Ask yourself, "What would I do if I had no fear?" Fear is the greatest enemy of passion. Fear, like worry, is generally much bigger in our minds than reality—false expectations appearing real. We all have fear, but only those who acknowledge and understand their fears can conquer them in pursuit of their passion.

__ **Create your own rituals.**

Rituals strengthen connections among those involved in the ritual and make them feel special for belonging to the "tribe." More importantly, rituals strengthen your passion for the purpose behind the ritual. A personal ritual can be as simple as having a family dinner every Sunday, going on a weekly date with your spouse, celebrating milestone achievements instead of immediately moving on to the next goal, or starting each day by reading an inspirational quote.

__ **Align your actions with your values.**

Sometimes our intentions cloud our perceptions of our values. Have you ever heard someone say, "I meant to tell her how important she was to our team before she left," or, "I intended to volunteer last weekend," or, "I meant to vote this past election," or, "I intended to keep my commitment, but. . ."? As we said earlier, the truth is that we judge ourselves by our intentions, but others judge us by our actions. Our actions are the real test of what we value. Take an honest look at your actions to see what you really value. If they are not in sync, either change your actions or change your values so you can live authentically.

— **Use your words to *change* your situation, not to describe it.**

The moment you speak something—good or bad—you give birth to it as an idea, an expectation, a desire. You have planted a seed that will, sooner or later, grow into the results you will reap. When you're feeling disheartened, don't tell people how you feel—tell them how you *want* to feel. By controlling what you say and how you say it—that is, using positive words with enthusiasm—you help change your physical and mental state.

— **Make an impact.**

Ask yourself before leaving the office each day, "Did I do something today that leaves a positive, lasting impact?" If the answer is no, stay until you do.

— **Build your BEST team.**

Your BEST team represents buddies who encourage success and truth. Choose your team wisely. Ensure that each member offers the energy, truth, and positive perspective you need to succeed. Connect with your BEST team, with individual team members and as a group, on a consistent basis. Learn from them and help them—it goes both ways. People who are passionate about something are willing to ask for things they need to help them achieve their goals, and people want to help those who have a passion for a purpose. So ask for help with confidence and respect. You will be amazed at what you will receive.

Close the Gap

Start closing the knowing-doing gap by reviewing the actions above and the at-a-glance summary below. Then, write down:

- One action you can take today to ignite your *team* passion

_____

_____

- One action you can take today to ignite your *personal* passion

_____

_____

PASSION At-a-Glance

- **Paint the picture**
  - Connect each job to a broader purpose.
  - Always answer the fundamental four questions.
  - Communicate proactively to avoid the silence spiral.
- **Give what you want**
  - Show uncommon respect with common courtesy.
  - Appreciate performance as well as the person behind it.
  - Encourage others with three simple words.
- **Value your values**
  - Build a solid foundation of values.
  - Define and manage behaviors that exemplify your values.
  - Make values-based decisions.
- **Create connections**
  - Ritualize your team.
  - Be accessible to your team.
  - Be who you are and nobody else.

PART V

Getting Started
... and **Sticking**
with It

21

Move Through Adversity

A s the old adage goes, "The best laid plans of mice and men often go awry." Changing market dynamics, internal challenges, and unexpected circumstances all have a way of disrupting our well-constructed plans. Even great plans that are thoroughly adhered to are not immune to encountering obstacles along the way. Most great stories of victory are, in actuality, great stories of overcoming adversity. At some point, virtually every team and organization experience adversities of some type: economic hardships, loss of a major customer, lack of funding, failed partnerships, new regulations that neutralize a competitive advantage, natural disaster, the death of a team member or a team member's loved one, reductions in the workforce and so on. We intentionally used the word "move" in this chapter's title because adversity has an uncanny knack of immobilizing us. Therefore, it's critical to keep moving through it. Otherwise, it's all too easy to get stuck in the muck and mire of adversity.

We suggest three steps to help you move through adversity and on to victory. First, **take stock of what was lost or has changed and have gratitude for what remains.** When we experience a significant setback, we tend to think that all is lost, but this is rarely the case. Once you have rationally and objectively assessed the negative ramifications of the situation, search for the positives and express your gratitude for them.

The value of taking stock and moving through challenges is exemplified by Anthony Robles. Even with two undefeated seasons and two high school state wrestling titles under his belt, Robles was not heavily recruited by colleges. So he felt he had something to prove in the college wrestling scene once he joined Arizona State University's team. And prove himself a worthy competitor is what he did. Robles won the NCAA Division I wrestling championship in 2011, capping off a perfect 36 and 0 season. En route to victory, he focused on doing amazing things with what he had. He didn't worry about what he did not have—one leg.

Anthony Robles was born with just one leg. As a kid, he hated his prosthetic leg, so he never used it. Everything he did—including playing basketball and football—he did on one leg. His freshman year in high school, Anthony joined the wrestling team. He lost virtually every match that first year. Then, with the help of his coach, he began adapting his strategy and style to fit what he did have, like incredible upper body strength. And before long, he was winning.[1]

Robles moved through the adversity of having only one leg in large part by focusing on what he had rather than what he had lost. When he received the 2011 Jimmy V ESPY Award for Perseverance, he said, "[My mother] taught me to never let what I cannot do interfere with what I can do. She didn't protect me from pain and failure because she knew it would make me stronger." He concluded his acceptance speech with this message: "Every soul who comes to earth with a leg or two at birth must wrestle his opponents knowing it's not what is, but what can be that measures worth. Make it hard, just make it possible, and through pain, I won't complain. My spirit is unconquerable. Fearless, I will face each foe for I know I am capable. I don't care what's probable, through blood, sweat, and tears I am unstoppable."[2]

The second step for moving through adversity is to **convert turning points into learning points.** Use challenges and obstacles as opportunities to improve, learn, grow, rebuild, or test your character or faith. The road to victory is rarely smooth. There will be detours and barriers along the way. Winning leaders and teams choose to grow past their challenges rather than use them as excuses to stop or to lower their sights.

Jay Myers knows all about growing past challenges and converting turning points into learning points. In fact, Myers could be a "poster child" for overcoming adversity. After growing a division of a telecommunications company from zero to $5 million in revenues, he was fired. At a key turning point in his life, Jay decided not to return to corporate America and instead founded Interactive Solutions, Inc. (ISI), a company specializing in the then-fledgling videoconferencing market. But the investors he had worked so hard to round up quickly pulled out of the deal; so he took on a partner. And thank goodness he did, because not long after launching the company, doctors discovered Jay had a melanoma. Fortunately, he recovered. However, his relationship with his partner didn't fare well, and they parted ways, leaving Jay with the company but also a load of debt.

For the next few years the company prospered, and Jay dug his way out of debt. Then, suddenly, Jay's brother, whom he was very close to and who handled the company finances, passed away. Jay hired a woman to handle the company's accounting and finances in his brother's absence. Little did he know that while he was grieving the loss of his brother, the woman was embezzling hundreds of thousands of dollars from the company, nearly forcing ISI into bankruptcy. Once again, Myers and his team pulled themselves up by their bootstraps and persevered. In his book, *Keep Swinging: An Entrepreneur's Story of Overcoming Adversity and Achieving Small Business Success* (Morgan James Publishing, 2007), Myers writes, "In thinking about what I had learned from the experience, I felt like it all happened for a reason. The experience has changed me, has changed the way I run my business." [3]

During the last economic recession, Jay faced another turning point when the company experienced a revenue decline for the first time in its 13-year history. Employees were anxious about the future of the company and worried about the possibility of losing their jobs. Myers says, "I once heard that 'some of the greatest opportunities in business come from moments of great distress,' and it seemed to me that with all the turmoil in the world, [we] might have an opportunity to do something our competition and others were not doing."

After much analysis and discussion, Myers and his team decided to "double down" and aggressively expand the business. They adhered to their plan, and it paid off in a big way—sales more than doubled in just a few short years.

Adversity should refine us, not define us. While Jay Myers needs no more challenges, he used challenges to learn and grow. Adversity seems to make Myers and his team stronger. In fact, Interactive Solutions was recently named one of the fastest-growing companies in the United States and made *Inc.* magazine's 500/5000 list for 2012, the seventh time it has made the list since 2001. A plaque in Jay Myers's office seems to echo his response to adversity: "Never, never, never give up." [4]

The third and final step for moving through adversity is to **plan for the future, but live in the present.** Don't obsess about yesterday, and don't be seduced by the promise of tomorrow. When we are in the midst of adversity, it's easy to say, "Once we get through this, then we will get back to our plan." With that mentality, we mortgage away our future by waiting until problems blow over and things get back to "normal." But what if things never get back to normal?

The catastrophe that befell Cantor Fitzgerald provides us with a poignant example of a leader who planned for the future but lived for the present. Cantor Fitzgerald was the largest wholesale financial services company in the world, handling about 25 percent of the daily transactions in the world's multitrillion-dollar treasury securities market. With 2,200 employees worldwide and 960 in New York, it was at the heart of the financial markets—the place where financial giants traded with each other.

On September 11, 2001, Cantor Fitzgerald chairman and CEO Howard Lutnick was late getting to work because he was accompanying his 5-year-old son to his first day of kindergarten. As he was leaving the school, Lutnick got a call telling him that the World Trade Center had been hit by a plane. He later remembered seeing the smoke from the burning buildings as he drove toward the city. "I just had to get down there as fast as I could . . . to make sure my people were getting out." [5]

When he arrived, people were streaming out of One World Trade Center. As he got closer to the building, he began grabbing people and asking them, "What floor are you on?" Cantor Fitzgerald occupied floors 101 through 105 of the building. Tragically, his employees' escape route was cut off when the plane ripped through the building on the lower floors. There was no way out.

Cantor Fitzgerald lost 658 employees that day, more than any other organization involved in the disaster, including the New York Fire and Police departments. Almost all of its stock and bond traders, as well as the accounting, human resources, and legal departments were killed, including Lutnick's brother and closest friend, Gary. The company was decimated in every sense of the word.

The Cantor Fitzgerald employees who perished that day had more than 1,500 children combined. Yet having lost more than two-thirds of his people and all of his physical assets, Lutnick had no choice but to stop paying deceased employees within days after the tragedy. There simply wasn't enough money. Lutnick understood the harsh reality— he could best help victims' families in the long run by getting the company back on its feet. On September 19, Lutnick pledged to distribute 25 percent of the company's profits for the next five years to employees' families and committed to paying for 10 years of healthcare. Cantor Fitzgerald fulfilled its promise, paying out a total of $180 million in profits through September 2006 and continuing healthcare coverage through October 2011.

While the tremendous loss of life was almost unbearable, maintaining stability in the country's and the world's financial markets was crucial in the days and weeks after 9/11. In a speech several days after the attack, Lutnick made these comments: "We will not allow this tragedy to sway us from our path—while we grieve, we intend to persevere. We remain confident that our systems and technology will perform as our customers have come to expect."[6] True to his word, the company's trading markets were back online within a week.

Lutnick lived a lesson for all of us. In the face of adversity, he methodically planned for the future while focusing on the present. As a result, Cantor Fitzgerald persevered through, and came back from, the worst of all circumstances. It has not only survived, but is once again a thriving leading financial services firm in the equities and fixed income markets.

Those who have survived life's adversities will tell you that a survival experience is an invaluable gift, because in adversity you get to know who you really are. There is a saying in the Tibetan language: "Tragedy should be utilized as a source of strength." Sooner or later, we all will face some form of adversity. Prepare your plan, your mind, and your team now for any challenges that might come in the future. Then, should adversity strike you or your team, follow the three steps, keep moving, and write your victory story.

Press on . . . your defining moment may arrive just when you feel surrounded by adversity.

DAVID COTTRELL, LEADERSHIP AUTHOR

22

Start Small to Finish Big

The key to finishing big is to start small. Big achievements like running a marathon, introducing a new product, or exceeding a hefty sales goal all start with one small step. Consistent "baby steps" lead to *big* places.

Starting small involves sharpening your focus, building your competence, and igniting your passion a little more each day. It's about using the multiplier effect of the adherence equation to your full advantage. (The graphic below provides a reminder of the success factors that drive each component.) The small steps you take today will have a big impact tomorrow.

Take Inventory, then Take Action

Winners understand the importance of continuous learning. They use life as their classrooms. They search for best practices everywhere. They watch the people around them. They realize that they can gain understanding about the art of adherence from a speaker at a professional association meeting, a pastor, a fellow leader, a mentor, a father-in-law, a child, a Little League coach, or a particularly helpful salesperson at a local department store. Winners are constantly observing, reading, asking, listening, and learning. Successful leaders also know that the pursuit of *self*-knowledge is at the core of their abilities to adhere to their plans. They are keenly aware of their natural strengths as well as their weaknesses.

Knowing yourself and your team yields practical wisdom that has a real impact on results. Despite the popular notion to the contrary, wisdom has little to do with age or experience. Learn as much about yourself and your team as you possibly can. **Your greatest liability is the one you are unaware of.** Furthermore, your strengths can't benefit you if you don't know how to leverage them. So stop right now and take a moment to complete the quick online adherence assessment (link below). You will receive real-time feedback that will help you immediately in two ways. First, the assessment will identify your starting point by measuring your current level of adherence. Second, it will identify areas you should address to improve your adherence. You can also send it to your team and receive a team score.

Adherence Assessment
www.theLgroup.com/StickwithIt

ADHERENCE At-a-Glance

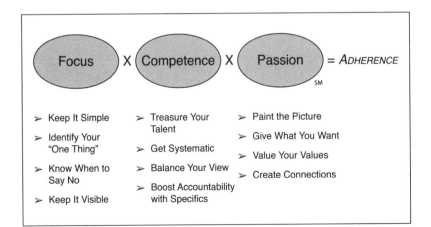

Once you have completed the adherence assessment, take three small steps to start building big results:

1. Review your adherence component subtotal scores and identify where you have the biggest opportunity for improvement. Is it focus, competence, or passion? Within that component, find the specific statement that you rated lowest. This is a good starting point for improving adherence. Go back and reread the section of the book that corresponds to your weakest component, paying close attention to the chapter that addresses the specific success factor you rated the lowest.

2. Identify your strongest adherence component from your subtotal scores. Think about ways you can use that strength to improve your adherence even more. Also consider ways you can leverage that strength to help you build other success factors that may need some work.

3. Keeping in mind that winning leaders start with themselves and build personal adherence before trying to build their teams' adherence, commit to one action you can take in the next 24 hours to start improving your personal adherence. If the assessment indicated that your team's focus is low, examine your personal focus. If your team's competence is subpar, check your own competence. If your team's passion is faltering, look at your personal passion for your work. Whatever action you take, it must start with you. For example:

- I will identify my one thing each week to sharpen my focus.
- I will identify three things I can stop doing so I can refocus my time on the vital few tasks.
- I will establish a meeting rhythm to ensure that my team is focused on the most important things.
- I will measure leading indicators of my performance to boost accountability for results.

- I will convert my thoughts of appreciation into acts of appreciation at least once a day.

If you haven't done so already, take your first small step right now and take the online adherence assessment. Just one small step will start you on your adherence journey.

From Actions to Habits

Once you have committed to action, turn your action into a habit. Here's why: Do you remember the first time you got behind the wheel of a car? Every action was intentional and conscious—you buckled the seat belt, checked the mirrors, put your foot on the brake, shifted out of park into drive, looked in all directions, gently stepped on the gas, and so on until you finally reached your destination with a big sigh of relief (for you and your parents). Now can you recall the last time you pulled up to your home, and as you shifted the car into park, you thought to yourself, "How in the world did I get here? I don't remember driving home." This experience is a direct result of your once-conscious actions becoming subconscious. You were operating on "autopilot," the sign of a well-ingrained habit. Habits are formed when the brain takes a shortcut and stops actively thinking about the decision being made. That's why we can drive home without consciously thinking about it.

Turning your small steps into positive habits will lead to big results. If you can put your ability to stick with your plan on autopilot, it will propel you to victory. It takes 21 days of repeated action and reinforcement to nurture a new habit, and the more frequently a new behavior occurs, the stronger the habit. Remember: Start small. You want to become a high achiever, so choose your one action carefully and then repeat it every day for at least 21 days. It is better to make fewer commitments and keep them than to load up on commitments and increase the chances that you will falter. We need to be laserlike with our commitments so we can more easily convert them into habits. The art of adherence is relatively simple once we do the hard work of forming positive habits—habits like maintaining a meeting rhythm, measuring leading indicators, using the 3 x 3 x 3 interviewing process, showing appreciation for at least one team member each day, reinforcing your team rituals, or using specific language when you set expectations.

The process of creating a new habit is a lot like a lunar voyage. The distance to the moon and back is about half a million miles. A spacecraft uses more energy in the first few minutes and miles of travel than in the remaining days and half a million miles because gravity is greatest near the Earth. It takes tremendous thrust to break free of Earth's gravitational pull. But once a rocket does break free, it takes relatively little energy to power the rest of the voyage. This is what it's like for us to either break old habits or create new ones. The greatest amount of energy and effort is required in the first 21 days as we try to escape the forces that want to pull us back to our old, comfortable ways. But after that, the energy and focus necessary to perform the new habit drops considerably. It becomes second nature, much like driving a car.

Winners do the things that others don't like to do. Legendary college football coach, Paul "Bear" Bryant said, "It's not the will to win, but the will to prepare to win that makes the difference." So put in the effort to turn your committed action into a habit. Then come back to this book, commit to another action that will improve your adherence, and create another positive habit from that action. Take small steps, one at a time, accumulating the victories and confidence that will build momentum. Each new positive habit will propel you farther on your adherence journey.

Stick with It

As we show early in the book, winning is more about executing with excellence than having a great strategy. As the famous U.S. general (and Olympic pentathlete) George S. Patton once said, "A good plan executed today is better than a perfect plan executed next week."

Sticking with your plan is simple but certainly not easy. There is nothing accidental about adherence. We can't expect to win by waiting around for "big things to happen," "the right team to be in place" or "the market to cooperate." As our good friend Ron Rossetti, associate vice president in the trial division of Nationwide Insurance, likes to say, "Awesomeness is never accidental." It's true—short-term wins might be accidental, but lasting success never is.

A solid plan, hard work, and a positive attitude yield winning results sooner or later. Adherence requires action, but it also requires patience. Being patient is not the same as being passive. Patience involves preparing to win and taking the necessary actions knowing that your actions might not yield immediate, visible results. Do you remember the example of the Indian Thorny bamboo plant from earlier in the book? Consider the patience required to nurture the bamboo seed, day in and day out, for two years while it develops its unseen, underground root system. Then recall what happens once it finally breaks through the soil—it can grow up to 100 feet in a month.

All the leaders and success stories we feature in this book have impatiently pursued their plans while patiently waiting for their efforts to take root. In every case, their adherence to their plans brought them victory. That same approach would serve each of us well. Have faith that your plan will work, and then get to work on it. Every day, execute with excellence as if you are already in the winner's circle. Keep pushing, keep learning, keep measuring, keep improving, keep believing. That's the art of adherence.

Mark your calendar for six months from today. When that date arrives, go online and retake the adherence assessment. If you have diligently followed the steps and applied the tools we describe in this book, your adherence will grow rapidly—just like the bamboo seed.

You don't have to be winning to get started, but you do have to get started to win. So get started today... and stick with it!

Winning Tools

Chapter	Title	Tool
Part I	The Art of Adherence	
4	Start with Strategy	Six simple questions template
Part II	Focus	
6	Keep It Simple	80/20 principle worksheet
8	Know When to Say No	4D task log
9	Keep It Visible	Communication plan sample
Part III	Competence	
11	Treasure Your Talent	Top 10 employee selection mistakes . . . and solutions
11	Treasure Your Talent	4 steps for winning coaches
12	Get Systematic	Idea tracker template
13	Balance Your View	Balanced scoreboard sample
13	Balance Your View	Scoreboard review process
14	Boost Accountability with Specifics	Accountability tracker
Part IV	Passion	
18	Value Your Values	Converting values to behaviors worksheet
19	Create Connections	Rituals worksheet
Part V	Getting Started . . . and Sticking with It	
22	Start Small to Finish Big	Adherence assessment. (Complimentary individual and team assessments).

Download Winning Tools here
www.theLgroup.com/StickwithIt

Reinforcement Resources
5 Ways to Reinforce *Stick with It*

1. **Strategic Planning & Execution Consulting**
   We work with you to create a simple, compelling plan, and then we help you adhere to it . . . and win!

2. **Keynote Presentation**
   Invite authors Lee J. Colan or Julie Davis-Colan to speak at your next meeting. Their passion and enthusiasm create energizing and engaging presentations. Your team will receive practical, powerful tools that they can put to work right away.

3. **Workshop**
   Based on *Stick with It*, this fast-paced, interactive workshop helps your team close the knowing-doing gap. Your team will be ready to sharpen focus, build competence, and ignite passion. Facilitated by one of the authors or a certified facilitator. Also available in Spanish.

4. **Training Resources**
   These professionally designed training resources equip your internal staff to confidently deliver anything from a lunch and learn to a full-day workshop. Includes dynamic slide show; detailed facilitator guide with speaking notes, exercises, stories, and tools; participant guide packed with practical tips and templates.

5. **Complementary Adherence Assessment**
   Individual assessment and team feedback reports.
   Visit www.theLgroup.com/StickwithIt

   For more resources, visit www.theLgroup.com or call 972-250-9989.

Notes

Chapter 1

1. FranklinCovey. *FranklinCovey Survey Reveals Top 3 New Year's Resolutions for 2008: Eliminate Debt, . . . Reuters.* 18 Dec. 2007. 17 June 2012. http://www.reuters.com/article/2007/12/18/idUS132935+18-Dec-2007+BW20071218.
2. Lauren Keller Johnson. "Execute Your Strategy—Without Killing It." *Harvard Management Update,* December 2004.
3. Robert Kaplan and David Norton, *The Strategy Focused Organization* (Boston, MA: Harvard Business School Press).
4. Nader Srouji, "Strategy Execution Challenges: A Behavioral Approach," *A Middle East Point of View,* November 2010, pp 23–25.
5. Booz & Company. *The Heat Is (Back) On: CEO Turnover Rate Rises to Pre-Recession Levels, Finds Booz & Company Annual Global CEO Succession Study. Booz.com.* 24 May 2012. 18 June 2012. http://www.booz.com/global/home /press/article/50560531.
6. Ram Charan and Geoffrey Colvin, "Why CEOs Fail," *Fortune,* June 21, 1999.
7. "CEO Challenge 2007—Top 10 Challenges," report by Conference Board Inc., New York, October 2007.
8. Lawrence G. Hrebiniak, *Making Strategy Work: Leading Effective Execution and Change* (Upper Saddle River, NJ: Wharton School Publishing, 2005).
9. www.haygroup.com/fortune/downloads/2012-FORTUNE-Lighting-the-path-to-success.pdf.
10. www.haygroup.com/fortune/downloads/2012-FORTUNE-Lighting-the-path-to-success.pdf
11. Stephen Taub, "Closing the Strategy-to-Performance Gap." CFO.com. CFO, February 22, 2005. online. 28 Aug. 2012. http://www.cfo.com/article .cfm/3686974.

Chapter 2

1. http://www.etymonline.com/index.php?allowed_in_frame=0&search=adhere& searchmode=none.
2. http://www.velcro.com/About-Us/History.aspx.
3. Alan Chodos, "February 9, 1990: Death of George de Mestral," *APS News,* February 2004; 13:2.

Chapter 3

1. Geoffrey Colvin, "America's Most Admired Companies," *Fortune*, February 21, 2000.
2. Ibid.
3. Mark Royal and Alan Wolfson, "Strategy Implementation: Lessons from Most Admired Companies," *Hay Insight Connections*, July 2002, p 4.

Chapter 4

1. Jennifer Pritchard, personal interview, August 14, 2012.

Chapter 5

1. "Living Well." *IU.edu.* Indiana University, 7 July 2012. http://newsinfo.iu.edu /news/page/normal/2838.html.

Chapter 6

1. Warren E. Buffett. "The Superinvestors of Graham and Doddsville." Speech. Columbia University. 1984. http://www.tilsonfunds.com/superinvestors.html
2. Gunter Rommel and Jurgen Kluge, *Simplicity Wins: How Germany's Mid-sized Industrial Companies Succeed* (Boston, MA; Harvard Business School, 1995).

Chapter 7

1. Peter Bregman. "How (and Why) to Stop Multitasking." *Blogs.hbr.org .Harvard Business Review, 20 May 2010. 8 July 2012.*
2. http://www.monitortalent.net/videos/technology-organization-people /sherry-turkle/merits-unitasking?category=All&page=6.
3. David Feinberg, personal interview. July 6, 2012.

Chapter 8

1. Jeffrey A. Krames, *What the Best CEOs Know: 7 Exceptional Leaders and Their Lessons for Transforming Any Business* (New York: McGraw-Hill, 2003).

Chapter 9

1. FranklinCovey. *New FranklinCovey Focus Solution Helps Employees Focus and Execute on Highest Priorities. TheFreeLibrary.com.* 13 Mar. 2003. 10 July 2012. http://www.thefreelibrary.com/New+FranklinCovey+Focus+Solution+Helps+E mployees+Focus+and+Execute+on...-a098698584.
2. Melissa Reiff, personal interview, July 6, 2012.
3. Ibid.
4. Cindy Lewis, personal interview, May 19, 2010.

5. Mark Blinn, personal interview, July 10, 2012.
6. Elaine Agather, personal interview, July 10, 2012.
7. Alvin Silverstein and Virginia Silverstein, *World of the Brain* (New York: William Morrow, 1986).

Chapter 10

1. http://www.biography.com/people/dave-thomas-9542110. Accessed 9-17-12.
2. Brian Tracy, *Eat That Frog!: 21 Great Ways to Stop Procrastinating and Get More Done in Less Time*, 2d ed. (San Francisco, CA: Berrett-Koehler Publishers; 2007).

Chapter 11

1. Hay Group, "Lighting the Path to Success," *Fortune*, 2012. p. 15, http://www.haygroup.com/fortune/downloads/2012-FORTUNE-Lighting-the-path-to-success.pdf.
2. Ibid., p. 12.
3. W. F. Cascio, *Managing Human Resources: Productivity, Quality of Work Life, Profits*, 7th ed. (Burr Ridge, IL: Irwin/McGraw-Hill, 2006). T. R. Mitchell, B. C. Holtom, and T. W. Lee, "How to Keep Your Best Employees: Developing an Effective Retention Policy," *Academy of Management Executive*, 2001, vol. 15, pp. 96–108.
4. Sandra Miles and Glynn Mangold, (2005), "Positioning Southwest Airlines through Employee Branding," *Business Horizons*; 48:6, pp. 535–545.
5. Greg Brown, personal interview. June 19, 2012.

Chapter 12

1. Andrew Levi, personal interview. July 3, 2012.
2. C. Pateand H. Platt, *The Phoenix Effect* (New York: John Wiley & Sons, 2002).

Chapter 13

1. Joe McKendrick. "How Steve Jobs Earned His MBWA Degree (Management By Walking Around)." *SmartPlanet.com*. 23 Nov. 2011. 12 Aug. 2012. http://www.smartplanet.com/blog/business-brains/how-steve-jobs-earned-his-mbwa-degree-management-by-walking-around/20157.
2. Bob Bunker, personal interview, Oct. 17, 2012.
3. Andrew Levi, personal interview, July 3, 2012.
4. John Walker, personal interview, July 10, 2012.
5. Dean Carter, personal interview, June 15, 2012.

Chapter 14

1. Mike Barnes, personal interview, July 2, 2012.

2. Peter Gollwitzer, "Goal Achievement: The Role of Intentions," *European Review of Social Psychology*, vol. 4 (Hoboken, NJ: John Wiley & Sons Ltd., 1993)

3. Stephen Mansfield, personal interview, June 14, 2012.

4. Paul Spiegelman, personal interview, June 22, 2012.

5. Henry Evans, *Winning with Accountability* (Dallas, TX: CornerStone Leadership Institute, 2008).

6. Elaine Agather, personal interview, July 10, 2012.

Chapter 15

1. Michael Ross, *Ebby Halliday: The First Lady of Real Estate* (Dallas: Brown Books, 2009).

2. Ibid.

Chapter 16

1. Lee Colan, *Engaging the Hearts and Minds of All Your Employees* (New York: McGraw-Hill, 2009).

2. Q12 James K. Harter, Frank L. Schmidt, Emily A. Killham, Sangeeta Agrawal, "Q12® Meta-Analysis: The Relationship Between Engagement at Work and Organizational Outcomes," (Omaha, NE: Gallup, Inc., 2009), p 3.

Chapter 17

1. Tom Rath, and Donald O. Clifton, *How Full Is Your Bucket?* (New York: Gallup, 2004).

2. Greg Brown, personal interview, June 19, 2012.

3. Charles Plumb. "Packing Parachutes." *Insights into Excellence*. Executive, 1993.

Chapter 18

1. Sharon Goldstein, personal interview, May 22, 2012.

2 Barry Davis, personal interview. July 9 2012.

Chapter 19

1. Karen A. Jehn, and Priti Pradhan Shah, "Interpersonal Relationships and Task Performance: An Examination of Mediation Processes in Friendship and Acquaintance Groups." *Journal of Personality and Social Psychology*, vol. 72, no. 4, 1997, pp. 775–790.

2. Susan Ellingwood, "The Collective Advantage," *Gallup Business Journal*. Accessed 20 Sept. 2012. http://businessjournal.gallup.com/content/787/the-collective-advantage.aspx.

3. Mac Anderson, and Lance Wubbels, *To a Child Love Is Spelled T-i-m-e: What a Child Really Needs from You.* (New York: Center Street, 2004).

4. David Feinberg, personal interview, July 6, 2012.

Chapter 20

1 Julie Neigher. "Taryn Rose Returns with New Comfort Fashion Shoe Lines." *Los Angeles Times.* 5 September 2010.

Chapter 21

1. Kalani Simpson, "Anthony Robles' 'Unstoppable' Drive." ESPN.com. N.p., July 12 2011. Web. September 27, 2012, http://sports.espn.go.com/espn/page2/story?id=6754598.

2. http://www.youtube.com/watch?v=ZD75y75xXU8.

3. Jay Myers, *Keep Swinging: An Entrepreneur's Story of Overcoming Adversity and Achieving Small Business Success.* Morgan James Publishing, 2007.

4. Lindsay Jones, "Keep Swinging." Mbq.com. Accessed September 25, 2012. http://www.mbqmemphis.com/core/pagetools.
php?pageid=14545&url=%2FMBQ-Inside-Memphis-Business%2FSeptember-2012%2FKeep-Swinging%2Findex.php%3Fcparticle%3D2%26siarticle%3D1&mode=print#;

5. "Cantor CEO Pledges Profits to Victims' Families." *CNN.* Cable News Network, 20 Sept. 2001. Accessed 25 Sept. 2012. http://edition.cnn.com/2001/US/09/20/vic.ceo.victims.families/.

6. ESpeed. *HOWARD LUTNICK, CHAIRMAN OF CANTOR FITZGERALD AND ESPEED, COMMENTS ON WORLD TRADE CENTER TRAGEDY. Espeed.com.,* 12 Sept. 2001. online. 28 Aug. 2012. http://www.espeed.com/articles/article09122001.htm.

Index

NOTE: Boldface numbers indicate illustrations

About the Authors

Lee J. Colan, PhD, is a high-energy leadership advisor, engaging speaker, and popular author. His 12 books have been widely read and applied by leaders at virtually every Fortune 1000 company and thousands of smaller organizations. Lee's cut-through-the-clutter advice, is anchored in his corporate leadership experience and consulting business over the past 25 years. His practical insights appear in hundreds of online and print outlets monthly.

Lee earned his doctorate in industrial/organizational psychology from George Washington University after graduating from Florida State University.

Julie Davis-Colan is cofounder of The L Group, Inc., a Dallas-based leadership consulting firm. She is an innovative business consultant and a compelling speaker. Julie turns vision and opportunity into a profitable reality. She spent 14 years marketing health initiatives to Fortune 500 companies at the American Heart Association national center. Julie's passion for leadership and life creates an infectious energy for clients and audiences.

Julie earned her master's degree from the Ohio State University College of Medicine in preventive medicine, after graduating from Florida State University.

To learn more visit www.theLgroup.com or call 972-250-9989.

The L Group equips
leaders at every level to WIN
by engaging their teams
and executing their plans.

THE **L** GROUP
Leadership at every level.

We help you WIN with...

Consulting: Our top-notch consultants
deliver cut-through-the-clutter insights
that drive results for your team.

Speaking: Engage your team with
passionate delivery and equip them
with practical tools.

Executive Advising: Our advisors help
senior executives boost organizational,
team and personal performance.

Resources: Rapid-read books, ready-
to-use Power Points, training kits,
audio programs, leadership assessments
and note cards, and posters to reinforce
your values.

Training: Rely on our certified
facilitators (English or Spanish
speaking) or use our just-add-water
training kits for internal delivery.